SALT & SHORE

SALT & SHORE

RECIPES FROM THE COASTAL SOUTH

SAMMY MONSOUR | KASSADY WIGGINS

weldonowen

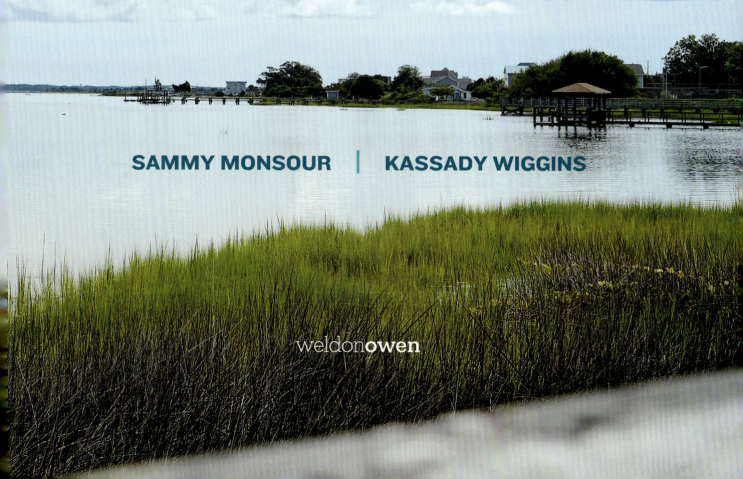

FISHING CHARTERS
LIVE BAIT
POLE RENTALS
FROZEN BAIT
KAYAK RENTALS
COLD BEER
WINE
LIVE MUSIC
EVERY SATURDAY

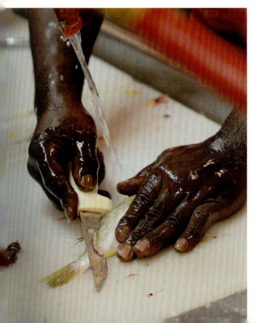

CONTENTS

12   Celebrating the Coastal South

LIBATIONS

- 18   Hibiscus Hoodoo
- 21   Punk Evans
- 22   Blue Bayou
- 25   *The Wonderful World of Algae*
- 26   Mezcalarita del Diablo
- 27   *Dehydrated Citrus*
- 28   Texas Two-Timer
- 29   Carolina Cherry Crush
- 31   The Whisky Thief
- 32   Voodoo Queen
- 35   Captain Creole
- 36   Shrunken Head(ache)
- 38   *Sea Love Sea Salt*
- 39   Savannah Slush
- 40   Caddywampus Punch
- 42   Lowcountry Cure
- 43   Houston Hoedown
- 45   Pawleys Island Palmer

ICE COLD

- 48   Creole Bay Scallop Ceviche
- 50   *Ceviche*
- 51   Fluke Ceviche with Ají Amarillo
- 52   Savannah-Style Cobia Crudo
- 54   Gulf Coast Amberjack Crudo
- 56   Key West Pink Shrimp Aguachile
- 58   Chip Shop Scalloped Potatoes
- 61   *Proper Caviar Service*
- 63   Carolina-Style Colossal Shrimp Cocktail
- 64   Cajun Lobster Cocktail
- 67   Nuoc Cham Crab Salad
- 68   Yellowfin Tuna & Watermelon Salad
- 69   *Why We Avoid Bright Red Tuna*
- 70   *On Oysters*

PINCHOS

- 79   Jamaican Jerk Conch Fritters
- 80   Louisiana Crawfish Hushpuppies
- 82   Catfish & Country Ham Croquetas
- 85   Crab & Green Chile Pimento Cheese
- 86   Peanut Chile Crisp–Butter Shrimp
- 88   *Sun Shrimp*
- 89   Marinated Mussels Toast
- 90   Lobster Rémoulade–Stuffed Piquillo Peppers
- 93   Smoked Mackerel Dip
- 94   *Tinned Fish*
- 97   Sunburst Smoked Trout Deviled Eggs
- 98   *Bottarga*
- 99   Spicy Swordfish & Chorizo Meatballs

HANDHELD

- 102   Swordfish Cubano
- 104   Caribbean Spiny Lobster Mulitas
- 107   The Miami
- 109   Fish 'n' Chips Submarine
- 110   Fish Shack Double Stack Deluxe
- 113   Louisiana Crawfish Roll
- 115   *Louisiana Crawfish Company*
- 116   Blackened Redfish Tacos with Hoppin' John Salsa
- 119   Fully Dressed Oyster Po'boy
- 121   Calabash-Style Rock Shrimp Sandwich

STOCK MARKET

- 124   Pan-Roasted Shellfish Stock
- 127   Lowcountry Shrimp & Grits
- 129   *Anchored Shrimp Co.*
- 130   Shellfish Gumbo Pot
- 131   *Gumbo*
- 133   Charleston Perloo

135 White Wine Fish Stock
136 Wahoo Brunswick Stew
137 Smoked Oyster & Butternut Squash Chowder
138 *Backyard Shellfish Boils*
139 All-Purpose Backyard Boil Stock
140 Lowcountry Shrimp Boil
140 Floribbean Clam Boil
140 Louisiana Crawfish Boil

FISH CAMP

144 *Seafood Frying Chart*
145 Calabash Style
146 Carolina Cornmeal
147 *Carolina Corn Revival*
149 Light & Crispy Beer Batter
150 Panko Crunch
152 *North Carolina Bonefish*
154 Cajun Yuca Steak Fries
155 Jamaican Jerk Tostones
159 North Carolina–Style Hushpuppies

CAST IRON

162 *The Southern Heritage of Cast-Iron Cookware*
165 *Caring for Cast Iron*
167 Whole Snapper with Autumn Succotash
168 Crawfish & Tasso Mac 'n' Cheese
170 Bacon & Beer Braised Clams
171 *Sapelo Sea Farms*
172 Pin Point Heritage Museum
173 Gullah Geechee Crab Fried Rice
175 Extra-Fancy Crab Cakes
176 Crab Gratin en Cocotte with Cajun Fried Saltines
179 Mahi-Mahi Curry Pot
180 *Smithey Ironware*
183 Perfectly Blackened Fish
184 Savory Oyster Bread Pudding

187 Smoked Trout & Sweet Potato Hash
188 Seared Sea Scallops with Middlins

HARDWOOD

192 *Mastering Hardwood Cookery*
193 *Hardwood Grilling*
194 Hickory-Roasted Monkfish Veracruzana
196 Harissa Charred Catfish
198 Carolina Gold Barbecued Grouper Cheeks
200 Wreckfish à la Parrilla
202 Tilefish with Pecan Salsa Macha
205 Backyard Charleston Oyster Roast
207 *Sea Island Forge*
208 *Pellet Grilling & Smoking*
209 Sweet & Spicy Fish Collars
211 Smoked Bluehouse Salmon Bravas
213 *Smoking Fish*
214 Coconut Unagi Barbecued Pompano
216 *Benne Seeds*
217 *Wood-Fired Oven Cookery*
219 Topneck Clams al Forno
220 *All Clams on Deck*
223 Salt-Crusted Black Sea Bass Escabeche
227 Oyster Bed Bienville with Texas Toast

SUNDRIES

230 Extra-Fancy Candied Yams
233 Lowcountry Cast-Iron Corn Bread
234 Pepsi-Cola Sea Island Red Peas
235 Coconut Ginger Collards
236 *George & Pink's*
237 Cacio e Pepe Grits
238 Slaw & Pickles
239 Seasonings
241 Rémoulades
244 Accoutrements

248 Index
254 Acknowledgments

Dedicated to our beloved "Beanie Girl," Loretta Lynn, who joyfully trotted by our side on countless coastal adventures throughout the creation of this cookbook.

Your love of the ocean and fine cuisine transformed ordinary moments into cherished memories. Endlessly kind, loving, and playful, you captured the hearts of those who were fortunate enough to have met you.

Though you've crossed the Rainbow Bridge, we imagine you running down the beach, stopping every so often for a bite of North Carolina-style hushpuppies, your tail "helicoptering" in delight.

Rest well, sweet girl. We love you so.

CELEBRATING THE COASTAL SOUTH

Salt & Shore presents a delightful assortment of sustainable recipes that showcase the unique flavors and culinary heritage of the coastal communities throughout the South. From the Atlantic Ocean to the Gulf of Mexico, the cuisine of the coastal South is expansive and dynamic, drawing from a rich and sordid history of colonization, exploration, and cultural exchange.

Beyond the delicious food and drinks, *Salt & Shore* highlights the interconnections between foodways, culture, history, and the environment. At its core, this book honors the individuals who have worked tirelessly to build a more sustainable and equitable food system in the South, including fishers, farmers, chefs, artisans, blacksmiths, docents, and community leaders. Our aim is to foster a deeper appreciation for the region by sharing some of our favorite stories about the people and places we've encountered during our wide-ranging exploration of the area.

For us, the humble dinner table is the world's greatest connector. We believe that good food and drinks are fundamental to happy living, bringing people together in a way that not much else can. Whether you're an experienced chef or just starting out, we invite you to savor and share these recipes with others and discover the joy of preparing meals and libations that connect us to one another and to our environment. We hope that our stories and recipes bring you closer to those around you and enrich your understanding of the communities, resilience, and sustainable living of the coastal South.

As you slowly flip through the pages of *Salt & Shore* and gain insight into the inspirations for our recipes, we invite you to keep an open mind toward what you may think Southern food *is*. Due to migration, immigration, climate, socioeconomic conditions, and even preferences, recipes are slightly altered from generation to generation. This is, from an anthropological perspective, how cuisine evolves. Recognizing this concept is important, so that when we look through the lens of what we think of as Southern cuisine, we understand that it's much more of a kaleidoscope than it is a microscope.

We invite you to join us in exploring the vibrant world of coastal Southern cuisine and beverages, where the sea meets the land, and the flavors are as diverse and colorful as the ocean itself.

Territory and Species

In the United States, the oceans, coastlines, fisheries, and sanctuaries are managed and conserved through a government agency called the National Oceanic Atmospheric Administration (NOAA). It uses the best scientific information available to keep our marine fishery resources in check, with the main objective being to maintain fish stocks important to commercial, recreational, and subsistence fisheries for the long haul.

In this book, we're focusing on species native to the NOAA Fisheries Southeast Region, which includes some of the best fishing spots in the country and encompasses fisheries in three areas: the Caribbean, the Gulf of Mexico, and the South Atlantic. These territories comprise federal waters from North Carolina to Texas along with Puerto Rico and the US Virgin Islands.

Commonly known as the coastal South, the region is made up of an interconnected series of waterways that embody a diverse array of aquatic environments, including salt marshes, oyster reefs, coral reefs, mudflats, and estuaries. It's the place we call home and is the source of inspiration for all that we do when it comes to food, beverage, and hospitality. We've traveled the length and breadth of this region over our lifetimes, and this book celebrates the communities,

cultures, and foodways we've discovered as well as the abundance of sustainable seafood species indigenous to the region.

The South offers a treasure trove of delicious wild-caught *and* farm-raised seafood, and we've challenged ourselves to showcase as many unique species as possible, while still making sure there are plenty of crowd-pleasers. The reality of sustainable sourcing is that availability is often determined by location, seasonality, and price. We've been mindful of this and have offered suggestions for suitable substitutions wherever possible.

Understanding Sustainable Seafood

As seafood eaters, we believe it's our duty to be aware of the impact our choices have on the environment and its inhabitants. We're committed to preserving the earth's precious natural resources and not taking more than we need. After all, the ocean isn't an all-you-can-eat buffet. It is our responsibility to work proactively toward the survival of the species we fish, farm, and forage—from freshwater trout to rope-grown mussels and even kelp. For us, sustainability means respecting the foundational values of balance and harmony in the natural world.

Our choices as consumers have a collective impact on our community, food system, and planet. When we make sustainable sourcing our north star, we transform our individual decisions into a powerful way of life, supporting healthier oceans and better practices throughout our food systems.

The ocean is a vast, complex system covering 70 percent of the earth's surface and accounting for 97 percent of our planet's water. From the symbiotic relationship between algae and coral to the otherworldly creatures of the deep, marine life depends on a delicate balance that modern society is disrupting. Today, our oceans face five major threats: overfishing, pollution, habitat destruction, warming, and acidification.

According to the United Nations Food and Agricultural Organization, 31.4 percent of global fish stocks are either fished to capacity or overfished. We have arrived at this point due to a range of unsustainable practices, including poor fisheries management, damaging catch methods, and pirate fishing fleets. Pollution has caused an ongoing man-made epidemic, with toxic amounts of nitrogen runoff from industrial agriculture and microplastics from single-use plastics endangering the health of our oceans. Greed and carelessness, from such practices as the clearing of mangrove forests for shrimp farming and the use bottom trawling to haul in more fish for less money, have often led to habitat destruction. Global warming is raising the temperatures of our oceans, with carbon emissions being the main cause. To top it all off, the global seafood industry is plagued by illegal fishing, product mislabeling, fraud, and even slavery. For these reasons, we can't stress enough how essential it is to demand transparency and traceability from our global seafood industry.

We have some huge challenges ahead, but we promise it's not all doom and gloom. We're happy to report that there are plenty of individuals and organizations on the water doing the good work needed to fix these issues and advance global sustainable seafood. The coastal South is home to countless activists dedicated to creating a cleaner and healthier tomorrow. Our hope is that this cookbook will connect you with the efforts of these individuals and organizations so you can make informed purchasing decisions and help support a sustainable future for our oceans.

Trusted Sourcing Resources

Sourcing sustainable seafood can be overwhelming. Knowing the species of your seafood, where it's from, and whether it was wild caught or farm raised will provide you with most of the information needed to determine its sustainability metrics. However, you'd need to be well-versed on environmental science and international food systems policy to decipher that data. That's why we established this list of trusted resources, broken down into four categories to make things easier to digest.

Eco certifications. These are globally recognized stamps of approval issued by independent organizations that have been accredited, licensed, or are supervised by the appropriate government authorities. The certifications are voluntary, involve ongoing inspection, and are supported by strong, well-managed commitments to sustainable practices. We look for eco certifications because they provide us with an assurance that the seafood we're buying meets most, if not all, of our sustainable sourcing criteria. The big seven that we've come to trust are the Marine Stewardship Council (MSC), Aquaculture Stewardship Council (ASC), Best Aquaculture Practices (BAP), Ocean Wise, FishWise, Friend of the Sea, and Fairtrade.

Sustainability ratings. These standards promote strong, science-based fisheries management and aquaculture practices by offering recommendations to help you choose seafood that has less impact on the environment. Our go-to guide for sustainability ratings is Monterey Bay Aquarium's Seafood Watch, a sustainable seafood advisory list that has been the global leader in this space for over two decades. Seafood Watch provides consumers with a comprehensive sourcing guide in the form of an extremely user-friendly app. Recommendations are reevaluated several times a year, based on the organic conditions of

life on our planet, so be sure to keep your app updated to reflect the most current sourcing suggestions.

Nongovernmental organizations (NGOs). Independent nonprofits that typically operate with an impact-driven mission, such as social or environmental justice, NGOs are the "on the ground" resources that provide us with guidance and leadership throughout our sustainable seafood missions. A variety of NGOs exist, ranging from local to statewide, national, and global. We recommend searching within your community to find organizations that you can meaningfully engage with, learn from, and support, such as an aquarium or coastal conservation center. National NGOs that we admire and continue to learn from include Oceana, Minorities in Aquaculture, Environmental Defense Fund, Marine Mammal Center, PangeaSeed Foundation, Oyster South, and SAGE (Seafood and Gender Equality).

Credible purveyors. In communities without an independently owned sustainable seafood market, we've had positive experiences at the seafood counters of Whole Foods and Costco, both of which are strongly committed to selling eco-certified seafood. If you're having trouble finding what you need at a brick-and-mortar retailer, we've compiled a list of vetted purveyors that we've purchased from in the past and, in some cases, even visited. Some are big-time and carry a wide variety, while others are mom-and-pop joints. Some are even farms that sell direct to the consumer, which we love. All ship across the continental United States.

With that being said, we find it important to be mindful of our carbon footprint. We acknowledge the resources consumed and the overall impact of purchasing food that's packed in Styrofoam coolers and shipped overnight on a jet to reach our doorstep void of spoilage. For what it's worth, we believe that awareness is an alias, and we cannot view sustainability as an all-or-nothing endeavor. Our list of trusted online retailers includes the following: Anchored Shrimp Co. (Brunswick, GA), Browne Trading (Portland, ME), Citarella (New York, NY), Fulton Fish Market (New York, NY), Louisiana Crawfish Company (Natchitoches, LA), Pike Place Fish Market (Seattle, WA), Sea to Table (various docks around the United States), Sterling Caviar (Elverta, CA), Sunburst Trout Farms (Waynesville, NC), Sun Shrimp (Pine Island, FL), and Wulf's Fish (Boston, MA).

LIBATIONS

AS EVERY GRACIOUS SOUTHERNER KNOWS, OFFERING a beverage to guests is a natural part of welcoming them into your home. Libations are an essential first step in planning and hosting a coastal Southern soirée. So after exchanging hugs and greetings, consider pouring your guests a fine cocktail to quench their thirst.

Crafting the perfect cocktail embodies the spirit of Southern hospitality like nothing else. Whether they're enjoying a lazy weekend brunch, cruising along the river, or rocking on a front porch while listening to the symphony of katydids and crickets, Southerners love just the right cocktail to suit the occasion.

Mixing cocktails is a fundamental art form of Southern culture. Even before the first recorded cocktail—the Sazerac—was created in New Orleans in the mid-1800s, Southerners had been using alcohol as a key ingredient in their elixirs and remedies. This chapter is a tribute to the South's rich history of imbibing, with a focus on coastal vibes, flavor profiles, and native ingredients. It's our way of sharing a welcoming embrace with you and your loved ones.

HIBISCUS HOODOO

Inspired by our dear friends and CheFarmers Matthew and Tia Raiford, this recipe is a tribute to their farming ancestry and the bounty of their land at Gilliard Farms in Brunswick, Georgia. As stewards of the Freshwater Gullah Geechee community, the couple works the same land that has been in Matthew's family since 1874. Among the many treasures they grow is hibiscus, which adds a delicate touch to this refreshing drink. For the ultimate Georgia experience, we highly recommend using gin made by Simple Man, a Georgia-based distillery that makes a variety of spirits (currently only available in Georgia) using fresh botanicals grown in the state. All of the botanicals used in this spirit are grown right on Gilliard Farms and play perfectly in this cocktail.

Fill a cocktail shaker with ice and add the gin, lemon juice, and hibiscus syrup. Cover and shake until well chilled. Strain over a large ice cube into a spritz glass. Top with sparkling wine. Garnish with the hibiscus flower and serve.

. . .

Hibiscus Syrup
Makes about 1½ cups

1 cup water
⅓ cup dried hibiscus flowers
1 cup organic sugar

In a small saucepan over medium heat, bring the water to a simmer. Remove from the heat, add the hibiscus flowers, cover the pan, and let steep for 5 minutes.

Immediately strain through a fine-mesh sieve into a bowl. Add the sugar to the hot infused liquid and whisk until dissolved. Transfer to an airtight container, label, and refrigerate. The syrup will keep for up to 3 weeks.

Makes 1 cocktail

1½ oz Simple Man or other floral-forward gin

¾ oz fresh lemon juice

½ oz Hibiscus Syrup

1 oz sparkling wine

Fresh hibiscus flower, for garnish

Cocktails

As you step into the world of making drinks, you might encounter some unfamiliar terms and measurements. Fear not, for a graduated jigger, a barspoon, a cocktail shaker, and a kitchen scale are the tools of the trade that will help you create consistent and delicious drink recipes. And don't worry if you don't have every ingredient in your pantry. Any of the more obscure ones, such as certain bitters, orgeat, falernum, and shrubs, are readily available from small businesses or major online retailers.

PUNK EVANS

Kassady here. The inspiration for this drink comes from my maternal grandfather's somewhat hyperbolic stories about his childhood and farm life in Missouri. Many of my papa's stories involve his buddy Punk Evans. He and Punk were teenage troublemakers—real rascals those two. The story goes something like this: they would sell watermelons on the side of a dirt road, and sometimes, if they didn't sell out, they'd go around smashing watermelons on people's front porches. So often when I think of watermelon, I imagine my grandfather as a teenager and his buddy Punk Evans causing a ruckus. This drink is a real crowd-pleaser; it is the most ordered cocktail at our restaurant in downtown LA, and I hope you'll find that's for good reason.

Fill a cocktail shaker with ice and add the vodka, lemongrass-ginger syrup, lime juice, and Cointreau. Cover and shake until well chilled. Strain into a rocks glass over the ice cubes and serve.

. . .

Lemongrass-Ginger Syrup
Makes 2 cups

5 oz fresh ginger, thinly sliced
1 oz lemongrass, from tender stalk portion, cut into small pieces
1½ cups organic sugar
½ cup water

In a blender, combine the ginger, lemongrass, sugar, and water and blend on high until the mixture is finely puréed and the friction from the motor begins to heat the mixture—you'll see steam begin to rise—2–3 minutes.

Strain through a fine-mesh sieve into a bowl, gently pressing against the solids with the back of a spoon to extract as much liquid as possible. Transfer to an airtight container, label, and refrigerate. The syrup will keep for up to 2 weeks.

. . .

Watermelon Ice Cubes

Put peeled watermelon flesh (seeds are fine to blend) into a blender and purée until smooth. Transfer to an ice-cube tray and freeze until solid.

Makes 1 cocktail

1½ oz Reyka vodka or other premium vodka

1 oz Lemongrass-Ginger Syrup

¾ oz fresh lime juice

¼ oz Cointreau

4 watermelon ice cubes

Icing Out Food Waste

Ice cubes aren't just for keeping your drinks cold anymore. They can add an extra dimension of flavor too. By using ice to repurpose your produce, you can enhance your drinks while also doing your part to combat food waste. Instead of tossing out those past-their-prime fruits and vegetables, juice them and then freeze the juice into flavorful ice cubes. And why stop at juice? Mix some cut-up fruit and/or herbs in water, freeze in an ice-cube tray, and then use the cubes to add a refreshing and unique twist to any beverage.

So the next time you find yourself with some extra produce on hand, pull out the ice-cube trays. You might just discover a new favorite way to savor the flavors of the season.

BLUE BAYOU

This rum-based sipper is more than just a drink. It's a zero-landfill cocktail that embodies the bold, innovative, and sustainable spirit of the South. Blue spirulina, a type of natural blue-green algae, is the star ingredient and is as fascinating as it is delicious. Sourced from controlled fresh- and saltwater environments, blue spirulina is a sustainable ingredient that provides a rich source of protein and other beneficial nutrients while also helping to reduce our impact on the environment.

And let's not forget about the cocktail itself. Its tropical flavors hit the spot and leave you feeling revitalized. By mixing a Blue Bayou, you can indulge in a delicious and innovative drink while also supporting sustainable practices. So let's raise a glass to a more sustainable South.

In a collins glass, muddle the kumquats. Fill the glass with ice. Fill a cocktail shaker with ice and add the rum, lemon juice, simple syrup, and spirulina. Cover and shake until well chilled. Strain into the glass. Garnish with the kumquat slices and serve.

• • •

Simple Syrup
Makes about 1½ cups

1 cup water
1 cup organic sugar

In a small saucepan over medium heat, bring the water to a simmer. Remove from the heat. Add the sugar and whisk until dissolved. Transfer to an airtight container, label, and refrigerate. The syrup will keep indefinitely.

Makes 1 cocktail

4 kumquats, halved (see Note)

2 oz Copalli white rum or other unaged rum

¾ oz fresh lemon juice

½ oz Simple Syrup

½ barspoon blue spirulina

Sliced kumquat, for garnish

Note: If kumquats aren't in season, a small handful of berries offers a wonderful substitute. The flavor profile will change, but the cocktail will be just as delicious. Garnish with seasonal berries of your choice.

THE WONDERFUL WORLD OF ALGAE

Using microalgae in drinks (and food) is really a win-win-win move. Algae are healthy for Mother Nature, healthy for us, and visually stunning to boot. When we consume algae, we contribute to a more sustainable world. And to be quite frank, algae are really fun to play with behind the bar. We believe that algae are some of the most exciting, unexpected, and underutilized ingredients when it comes to the beverage world. We use powdered microalgae (unicellular algae) in cocktails and nonalcoholic beverages alike to achieve vibrantly colored drinks with surprising health benefits.

If you're intimidated by the concept of using algae, don't be. You've most likely been enjoying them for years. If you're a sushi lover, the nori seaweed sheet wrapping your sushi roll is an alga (not all algae are seaweeds, but all seaweeds are algae). If you've come across a food label that reads "natural food coloring," it was most likely produced with algae. Have you ever walked into a juice or smoothie shop and seen spirulina and/or chlorella listed on the menu? Yep, those are algae too!

Most algae are plantlike aquatic organisms that can be as small as single-cell phytoplankton on top of water and as large as a one-hundred-foot-tall kelp blade. Different types of algae have different taste profiles, but the microalgae we use in beverages (blue spirulina, chlorella, and astaxanthin algae) have a neutral taste. They are some of our favorite ingredients to work with behind the bar and are readily available for purchase at your local health food store or from online retailers, including Walmart, Amazon, and Thrive Market.

Along with being extremely important to the health of our oceans, algae are very healthful for us to consume. Not all algae contain the same nutrients, so think of them like you do different vegetables in the grocery store. For instance, blue spirulina (seen in the Blue Bayou cocktail on page 22) is extremely high in protein and contains vitamins E, B_1, B_2, B_3, and B_9, whereas chlorella (used in the Pawleys Island Palmer on page 45) is a good source of fiber and of vitamins C, E, K_1, B_{12}, B_1, B_2, and B_6.

Thanks to their secondary pigments (phycobilins) that capture light energy and protect microalgae from harmful radiation, the beverages we concoct with algae are intense in color. And when we say intense, we mean it. You'd be hard-pressed to find an unnatural food dye that can give you the richness and brilliance of the colors that naturally occur in microalgae. One of the best parts is that a little goes a long way. Most (single-serve) cocktails that we make call for only 1/2 barspoon of any given alga. So next time you want to wow your guests, need an icebreaker, or would like to add some nutrients to your drink, reach for the algae!

MEZCALARITA DEL DIABLO

As you explore the pages of this book, you'll discover the incredible influence Mexican ingredients have had on Southern cuisine, and the same goes for Southern cocktails. The Mezcalarita del Diablo is a tribute to some of the bold flavors and ingredients that have made their way up from Mexico. This smoky and fiery twist on a classic margarita features mezcal, homemade ancho syrup, tangy lime juice, and a kick of ground chipotle. Whether you pair it with Blackened Redfish Tacos with Hoppin' John Salsa (page 116) or Caribbean Spiny Lobster Mulitas (page 104), or you're simply craving a heady and flavorful cocktail, this "deviled" drink is the perfect choice to quench your thirst. When buying a bottle of mezcal, we always reach for ones that are 43 percent ABV or higher. At that level, you can really begin to taste the terroir and the flavor nuances of the spirit.

Makes 1 cocktail

1½ oz Montelobos Espadín mezcal or other unaged (joven) mezcal

1 oz Ancho Syrup

¾ oz fresh lime juice

¼ oz Cointreau

Ground chipotle, for garnish

Dehydrated citrus, for garnish

Fill a cocktail shaker with ice and add the mezcal, ancho syrup, lime juice, and Cointreau. Cover and shake until well chilled. Strain over a large ice cube into a rocks glass. Sprinkle with the chipotle, garnish with the dehydrated citrus, and serve.

• • •

Ancho Syrup
Makes about 3 cups

1 oz whole ancho chiles (about 2 chiles)
2 cups water
1½ cups organic sugar

Preheat the oven to 375°F. Put the anchos on a small sheet pan and toast in the oven for 3 minutes. Let cool, remove the stems, tear the chiles in half, and drop the halves into a small saucepan.

Add the water to the pan, place over medium heat, and bring to a simmer. Remove from the heat, cover, and let steep for 1 hour.

Scoop up the chiles into a fine-mesh sieve held over the pan and, using the back of a spoon, gently press against the chiles to force out all the juices into the water, then discard the chiles. Add the sugar to the chile water and whisk until fully dissolved. Transfer to an airtight container, label, and refrigerate. The syrup will keep for up to 3 weeks.

DEHYDRATED CITRUS

Dehydrated citrus is one of our favorite garnishes for drinks. It has a crispy and chewy texture that tastes almost like candy, making it a pretty and flavorful accent. Plus, it's an easy way to cut down on food waste.

To make dehydrated citrus, preheat your oven to the lowest setting (usually around 175ºF or 200ºF). Line a sheet pan with parchment paper or a nonstick baking mat. Slice the citrus crosswise about 1/8 inch thick on a mandoline or with a sharp knife. Arrange the slices on the prepared sheet pan, spacing them about 1 inch apart.

Bake for 2 hours then rotate the slices 180 degrees and continue to bake. The dehydration process can take up to 5 hours, depending on the size and water content of the citrus. Once the citrus is no longer sticky to the touch, it's ready.

Once cool, dehydrated citrus will keep in an airtight container in a cool, dark cupboard for up to 1 year.

TEXAS TWO-TIMER

Whether you're in the mood for a refreshing summer sipper or a lively happy-hour cocktail, the Texas Two-Timer delivers. This cocktail packs a punch with each sip. Made with a blend of blanco tequila, Aperol, passion fruit purée, and lime juice, this drink is both sweet and tangy. The hint of dry bitterness from the Aperol perfectly balances the bold flavors, and the black lava salt rim adds a touch of earthy terroir to the mix. We've always been able to find passion fruit purée in the freezer section of our local grocer; simply thaw before making this cocktail.

Rub the rim of a rocks glass with a lime wedge, or dip rim of glass in simple syrup. Pour a small amount of salt onto a flat saucer. Gently roll the dampened edge in the salt to coat.

Fill a cocktail shaker with ice and add the tequila, lime juice, Aperol, simple syrup, and passion fruit purée. Cover and shake until well chilled. Add a large ice cube to the glass, strain the cocktail into the glass, and serve.

Makes 1 cocktail

Lime wedge and black lava salt, for rimming the glass

1½ oz El Tequileño blanco tequila or other blanco tequila

¾ oz fresh lime juice

½ oz Aperol

½ oz Simple Syrup (page 22)

½ oz passion fruit purée

CAROLINA CHERRY CRUSH

Unwind and relax after a long day in the sun with this nonalcoholic drink. Tart cherry juice not only provides a delicious tang but also promotes healthy sleep, thanks to its natural melatonin content. Lemongrass is believed to aid in digestion and boost immunity, and ginger can help reduce inflammation and settle an upset stomach. By turning limes that are on the edge of spoiling into ice cubes, you're actively reducing your food waste. Sit back and savor this delightful drink, and let the flavors transport you to a relaxed and rejuvenating coastal atmosphere.

In a collins glass, combine the cherry juice, soda water, and lemongrass-ginger syrup. Fill the glass with the lime ice cubes, stir gently, and serve.

• • •

Lime Ice Cubes

Cut limes into small pieces. (This is a great use for limes that are on the brink of being wasted.) Put the pieces into an ice-cube tray. Fill the tray with water and freeze until solid. This technique can be done with any citrus, and the ice is a good addition to any drink that benefits from a citrus accent.

Makes 1 drink

4 oz tart cherry juice

4 oz soda water, chilled

3/4 oz Lemongrass-Ginger Syrup (page 21)

Lime ice cubes

N/A Beverages

Permanently on the wagon or just taking a break from imbibing? Fear not! Just because you're not partaking doesn't mean you have to miss out on the fun. We believe in creating nonalcoholic drinks that are just as visually striking and delicious as their boozy counterparts. Throughout this section, we intentionally bring in ingredients from our cocktail recipes to help reduce food waste and provide non-alcoholic alternatives. So go ahead, indulge in a guilt-free beverage, and join in on the festivities!

THE WHISKY THIEF

Get ready to steal a sip of the bold and refreshing flavors of The Whisky Thief! This riff on the highball combines the smooth yet slightly smoky taste of Japanese whisky with the refreshing essence of cucumber, the subtle herbal notes of dill flower, and a hint of sea salt for a perfectly balanced and extremely bracing drink. Whether you're a whisky (or whiskey) enthusiast or your taste buds are simply in the mood for something lively, whip yourself up this inspired cocktail. When choosing a soda water, we suggest one with big bubbles. If you don't have a highball ice-cube tray, crushed ice works well too.

Spiral the cucumber ribbon around the inside of a highball glass. Drop highball ice into the glass. Add the soda water, whisky, cucumber syrup, and salt and stir gently with a barspoon to mix well. Garnish with the dill flower and cucumber flower (if using) and serve.

. . .

Cucumber Syrup
Makes about 2/3 cup

1 cup organic sugar
4 1/2 oz English cucumber, thinly sliced (about a 4-inch piece).

In a bowl, combine the sugar and cucumber and stir gently to mix well. Let sit at room temperature, stirring occasionally, until a syrup forms, about 30 minutes.

Strain through a fine-mesh sieve, gently pressing against the solids with the back of a spoon, into an airtight container, label, and refrigerate. The syrup will keep for up to 2 weeks.

Makes 1 cocktail

Cucumber ribbon, for garnish

4 oz soda water, chilled

1 1/2 oz Suntory Toki or other Japanese whisky

1/2 oz Cucumber Syrup

Pinch of sea salt

Dill flower and cucumber flower, for garnish (optional)

Cucumber Ribbon

Cut an English cucumber in half lengthwise. Using a vegetable peeler, and starting at one end of a cut side, cut a thin slice of cucumber from top to bottom.

VOODOO QUEEN

The Voodoo Queen is the epitome of a New Orleans tiki drink: strong, mysterious, enticing, and just a bit sneaky. You might have to search online for some of these ingredients, but we promise it's worth the extra effort to source them. Like many other tiki cocktails, this one calls for orgeat (specifically Creole orgeat) and falernum. Luckily, most high-end bottle shops carry falernum, and if your local one doesn't, don't be afraid to ask the shopkeeper to order a bottle for you. To truly elevate the flavor profile of this already delicious drink, we recommend using Creole orgeat from El Guapo, a company based in the heart of NOLA that makes its Creole orgeat with Louisiana pecans and sugarcane. Trust us, it's the secret ingredient that you don't want to miss.

Fill a cocktail shaker with ice and add the rum, lime juice, orgeat, falernum, and both bitters. Cover and shake until well chilled. Strain into your favorite tiki mug filled with crushed ice.

If you really want to go for the gusto and see fire, here's how you get there. Ream the lime half to release all the juice, then set the lime hull, open side up, on top of the cocktail. Add the overproof rum to the lime and ignite the rum with a stick lighter to create a flame. With your hand 8–10 inches above the flame, sprinkle a bit of cinnamon onto the flame and watch the fire dance. Blow out the flame before consuming the drink.

Makes 1 cocktail

1½ oz Appleton Estate or other Jamaican rum

½ oz fresh lime juice

½ oz El Guapo Creole orgeat

¼ oz falernum

4 dashes Bitter End Jamaican Jerk bitters

4 dashes El Guapo Polynesian Kiss bitters

½ lime, for garnish (optional)

½ oz overproof rum, for garnish (optional)

Ground cinnamon, for garnish (optional)

HANGOVER HELPERS

CAPTAIN CREOLE

This is no ordinary Bloody Mary. It's the embodiment of coastal Southern charm and flavor. The addition of poblano-infused vodka gives it a delightful twist, and when paired with a seafood garnish, it's nothing short of perfection. For the ultimate experience, we recommend using Bloody Mary mix made by Seaside Grown, a company based in South Carolina that sources tomatoes from a network of family-owned American farms. Whether you're treating yourself to a solo brunch or hosting a crowd, this drink is guaranteed to impress.

Rub the rim of a 16-oz glass with a lemon wedge. Mix together equal (small) amounts of seasoning and salt on a flat saucer. Gently roll the dampened edge in the seasoning-salt mixture to coat.

Add the vodka, hot sauce, and Bloody Mary mix to the glass. Stir with the celery rib to mix well. Add ice to fill the glass. Thread the tomato, oyster, and shrimp onto a cocktail skewer, garnish the glass, and serve.

. . .

Poblano Vodka
Makes about 3 cups

4 oz poblano chiles
1 bottle (750 ml) vodka

Cut the chiles into 1-inch pieces. In an airtight container, combine the chiles, along with their stems and seeds, and vodka and cap tightly. Let infuse at room temperature for at least 8 hours, shaking or stirring lightly every few hours to release the chile flavor. The longer the infusion time, the deeper the flavors. Taste and make sure the infusion is to your liking.

Strain through a fine-mesh sieve into a second airtight container, cap, and label. The infused vodka will keep in a cool, dark cupboard for up to 6 weeks.

Makes 1 cocktail

Lemon wedge, Lowcountry Boil Seasoning (page 239) or Old Bay Seasoning, and kosher salt, for rimming the glass

2 oz Poblano Vodka

4 dashes Sea Salt–Fermented Red Hot Sauce (page 247) or Crystal extra-hot hot sauce

4 oz Seaside Grown Bloody Mary Mix

1 celery rib

Cherry tomato, tinned smoked oyster, and cooked shrimp, for garnish

HANGOVER HELPERS

SHRUNKEN HEAD (ACHE)

Who says you can't mix tropical tiki flavors with a Bloody Mary? This recipe is a brunch twist on a classic tiki drink, blending the sweet tanginess of passion fruit and pineapple with the savory kick of a Bloody Mary. The addition of pineapple vodka gives it an extra boost to help you tackle even the toughest of mornings when you're trying to shrink a pesky headache. This potent elixir will also add some flair to your brunch spread.

Rub the rim of a 16-oz glass with a lime wedge. Mix together equal (small) amounts of coriander and salt on a flat saucer. Gently roll the dampened edge in the coriander-salt mixture to coat.

Add the vodka, passion fruit purée, lemon juice, lime juice, bitters, and Bloody Mary mix to the glass. Stir with the celery rib to mix well. Add ice to fill the glass. Skewer all garnishes, add the mint alongside, and serve.

. . .

Pineapple Vodka
Makes about 3 cups

1 pineapple
1 bottle (750 ml) vodka

Peel and slice the pineapple, then cut into 2-inch chunks. In an airtight container, combine the pineapple and vodka, making sure the pineapple is completely submerged in the vodka, and cap tightly. Let infuse at room temperature for at least 8 hours, shaking or stirring lightly every few hours to release the pineapple flavor. The longer the infusion time, the deeper the flavors. Taste and make sure the infusion is to your liking.

Strain through a fine-mesh sieve into a second airtight container, cap, label, and refrigerate. The infused vodka will keep for up to 4 weeks.

Makes 1 cocktail

Lime wedge, ground coriander, and kosher salt, for rimming the glass

2 oz Pineapple Vodka

¾ oz passion fruit purée

¼ oz fresh lemon juice

¼ oz fresh lime juice

3 drops El Guapo Polynesian Kiss bitters

4 oz Seaside Grown Bloody Mary Mix

1 celery rib

Pineapple slice, Luxardo maraschino cherry, kumquat, and lime wheel, for garnish

2–3 sprigs mint, for garnish

SEA LOVE SEA SALT

Sea Love Sea Salt produces high-quality sea salt that's hand harvested from local waters, filtered, solar evaporated, and packed, all in the beautiful town of Wrightsville Beach, North Carolina. Operated by Jeanette Philips and Jason Zombron, partners in life and in business, the company guarantees that its salt is 100 percent natural, which gives it a wonderful clean and pure taste. You'll love the coarse look and crunchy texture of the salt, and you can use it as larger crystals or break it down in your fingers for a finer finish. It's a magnificent finishing salt on everything from drinks to meats, salads, eggs, roasted vegetables, and even popcorn. In addition to its classic sea salt, Sea Love offers a variety of flavored blends. Try the dill pickle salt on a Bloody Mary rim or the citrus and guajillo blends in your margaritas.

SAVANNAH SLUSH

As beautiful and charming as it is, nobody can convince us that there is a hotter place on God's green earth than Savannah, Georgia, in August. It's a spot that can truly test your mettle. The heat is unforgiving, and the air feels like hot syrup. But fear not, weary traveler, we have just the thing to help you cool down and keep your sanity intact: the Savannah Slush. This one is perfect for strolling the streets and taking in the charming scenery. And if you're lucky enough to find some frozen Georgia or South Carolina peaches, it'll take your slush to the next level. To tie everything together, we recommend using Rhoot Man mango shrub, a delicious addition from veteran owner Sidney Lance's impressive lineup of shrubs. So take a sip, relax, and remember, cooler temperatures are just around the corner.

Rub the rim of a 16-oz glass with a lemon wedge. Pour a small amount of citrus sea salt onto a flat saucer. Gently roll the dampened edge in the salt to coat.

In a blender, combine the peaches, sugar, water, bourbon, shrub, and lemon juice and blend on high speed for 30 seconds, or until your desired consistency is achieved. Pour into the glass, garnish with the mint, and serve.

Makes 1 cocktail

Lemon wedge and citrus sea salt (preferably from Sea Love Sea Salt), for rimming the glass

2 cups frozen sliced peaches

2 tablespoons organic sugar

4 oz water

2 oz Maker's Mark bourbon or other Kentucky bourbon

1 oz Rhoot Man mango shrub

½ oz fresh lemon juice

2–3 sprigs mint, for garnish

CADDYWAMPUS PUNCH

Caddywampus may not be a commonly used term among the younger generation of Southerners, but it's one of our favorite colloquialisms. It's a fun and quirky word that perfectly captures the essence of something that's a little off-kilter. Here it is used to describe a drink that is meant to be shared with friends and enjoyed in good company. This fruity and slightly tangy punch combines sweet strawberries, smooth brandy, aromatic Peychaud's bitters, nutty Creole orgeat, and tart lemon juice for a nicely balanced taste. It's a great conversation starter and is sure to bring a little fun to any gathering. So grab a glass and share a toast with your loved ones.

Fill a large cocktail shaker with ice and add 2 oz brandy, 2 oz bitters, 2 oz orgeat, and 2 oz lemon juice. Cover and shake hard until well chilled. Repeat with the remaining ingredients. Strain into a punch bowl with at least a 40-oz capacity. Add ice to the bowl, then garnish the bowl with strawberries.

Garnish 4 rocks glasses with sliced strawberries and fill with ice. Invite guests to fill the glasses with punch.

. . .

Strawberry Brandy
Makes about 3 cups

3 cups strawberries, hulled and sliced
1 bottle (750 ml) brandy

In an airtight container, combine the strawberries and brandy and cap tightly. Let infuse at room temperature for at least 8 hours, shaking or stirring lightly every few hours to release the strawberry flavor. The longer the infusion time, the deeper the flavors. Taste and make sure the infusion is to your liking.

Strain through a fine-mesh sieve into a second airtight container, cap, label, and refrigerate. The infused brandy will keep for up to 4 weeks.

Makes 4 servings

4 oz Strawberry Brandy

4 oz Peychaud's bitters

4 oz El Guapo Creole orgeat

3 oz fresh lemon juice

Sliced strawberries, for garnish

Punch Bowls

There's just something exciting and enticing about a large-format cocktail in a punch bowl. Beautiful as the centerpiece, a full punch bowl will become the life of the party no matter where it is placed. It does a great job of bringing folks together, and using one as a vessel for preparing cocktails in advance means you can spend more time with your guests.

We always suggest using larger ice cubes in punch bowls. That way, the cocktails don't get watered down as your guests serve themselves throughout the gathering.

LOWCOUNTRY CURE

Kassady's Momma's Key lime pie is a legend in its own right. People have hounded us for the pie recipe for decades, and we can assure you the secret will never be spilled onto the pages of any cookbooks of ours. But now there's a cocktail homage to it, and it may be the closest anyone can get to a tantalizing slice without some serious buttering up to the Queen of Key Lime herself. This drink recipe is versatile, as it can be made with vodka, tequila, rum, bourbon, or as a mocktail, making it perfect for any occasion. We usually make it nonalcoholic and allow the guests to decide what type of spirit they'd like to add.

If using Key limes, cut them in half. If using regular limes, cut them into quarters. In a blender, combine the limes, coconut milk, and water and pulse for 10–15 seconds. If blended for any longer, the drink will start to taste bitter. Strain through a fine-mesh sieve into a pitcher or punch bowl.

Fill 8 rocks glasses with ice and garnish each glass with a lime wheel. At this point, the drink is still nonalcoholic. To make it into a cocktail, add 1½ oz of preferred spirit to each rocks glass and fill to the top with the cure mixture.

Makes 8 servings

12 Key limes, or regular limes

1 cup sweetened condensed coconut milk

6 cups water

8 lime wheels, for garnish

12 oz preferred spirit (optional)

HOUSTON HOEDOWN

Houston's culinary scene is renowned for its diversity and innovation, and the city's love affair with Vietnamese cuisine is a big part of that fame. This recipe pays homage to the deliciously complex flavors of Vietnam, with a heavy nod to the many refreshing coconut and kumquat drinks found there. Made with the water and meat of a young coconut, raspberries, tangy kumquats, hibiscus syrup, and a touch of sea salt, it offers a satisfying balance of sweet and tart flavors. We serve it in the hollowed-out young coconut for an added tropical touch.

Open the young coconut (see Note) and pour the coconut water directly into a blender. Using a spoon, scrape the insides of the coconut to remove the soft white meat and add it directly to the blender.

Add the raspberries, kumquats, hibiscus syrup, and salt to the blender and blend on high speed for 10 seconds, or until your desired consistency is achieved. Fill the coconut with crushed ice. Pour the contents of the blender into the coconut. Garnish with the mint, raspberry, and kumquat and serve.

Makes 1 drink

1 young coconut

6 raspberries, plus 1 more for garnish

5 kumquats, plus 1 more for garnish

½ oz Hibiscus Syrup (page 18)

Pinch of sea salt

2–3 sprigs mint, for garnish

Note: The easiest way to open a young coconut is with a long-handled cutter and mallet, a two-piece set you can order online. A few whacks of the mallet cuts a nice round hole in the top. Failing that, use a sturdy chef's knife to remove the coconut husk around the top, revealing the coconut shell, and then carefully cut across the top to create an opening.

PAWLEYS ISLAND PALMER

We're not here to pretend like we came up with the idea of mixing iced tea and lemonade. It's a timeless combination that's hard not to love. But why settle for basic flavors when you can easily create a homemade syrup that will elevate this classic drink to new heights? With just a few simple ingredients like fragrant lavender, earthy sage, and sweet honey, you can transform your drink into a sophisticated and refreshing beverage that's perfect for sipping on a warm day. And for an added boost of health benefits, why not sprinkle in some nutrient-rich chlorella? Trust us, your taste buds and your body will thank you.

In a 16-oz glass, combine the tea, lemon juice, lavender-sage syrup, and chlorella. Fill the glass with ice and stir gently until well mixed. Top with the soda water. Garnish with the lavender flower, sage leaf, and lemon wheel and serve.

• • •

Lavender-Sage Syrup
Makes about 2 cups

1 cup water
1 cup honey
¼ oz dried or fresh lavender
¼ oz dried or fresh sage

In a small saucepan over medium heat, bring the water to a simmer. Add the honey, stir until fully dissolved, and remove from the heat. Add the lavender and sage, cover, and let steep for 5 minutes.

Strain through a fine-mesh sieve into a heatproof airtight container, let cool, cap, label, and refrigerate. The syrup will keep for up to 6 weeks.

Makes 1 drink

5 oz brewed fair-trade black tea, chilled

2 oz fresh lemon juice

2 oz Lavender-Sage Syrup

½ barspoon chlorella

1 oz soda water, chilled

Fresh lavender flower, fresh sage leaf, and lemon wheel, for garnish

ICE COLD

BELLIED UP TO A RAW BAR WITH A TOWER FULL of ocean treasures is our happy place, and we know we're not alone in that sentiment. Raw-bar menus are light, crisp, healthy, and refreshing. But far too often, attempting to recreate platters of raw seafood preparations at home can feel intimidating. Although these preparations are often simple, they typically rely on strong technique and savvy sourcing knowledge. You'll find help to achieve both in this chapter, our comprehensive guide to all things raw, shucked, marinated, and served cold.

CREOLE BAY SCALLOP CEVICHE

Louisiana's "holy trinity" of celery, green bell pepper, and onion serves as a flavorful base for many Southern stocks and stews as well as other dishes. In this recipe, we showcase its ability to provide crunch and brightness by replacing the traditional bell pepper and yellow onion with Anaheim chile and green onion. With this simple swap, the dish takes on a vibrant fresh flavor while still honoring its Creole roots. Marinating the scallops with salt and fresh citrus juice denatures the protein, leaving it tender and packed with flavor. We can't get enough of bay scallops prepared this way, as it enhances their natural sweetness and gives them a refreshing kick. Mixing the ingredients *just* before serving is essential to retaining the full flavor and texture of the dish.

In a bowl, combine the scallops, lemon zest and juice, and 1 teaspoon kosher salt. Mix gently until the scallops are evenly coated, then pack the mixture into a storage container small enough to ensure all the scallops are submerged in liquid. Cover and refrigerate for at least 2 hours or up to 1 day.

Meanwhile, mix together the celery, Anaheim chile, green onions, parsley, and garlic, cover, and refrigerate until needed.

To serve, transfer the scallops and their juice to a bowl and add all the prepped produce along with the oil, guajillo chile (if using), and pepper. Gently fold together all the ingredients. Taste for seasoning and adjust with salt to your liking if necessary.

Transfer the ceviche to a chilled serving bowl and accompany with something crunchy—we love plantain chips—for scooping, snacking, and textural contrast.

Makes 2–6 servings

1 lb bay scallops, small muscle band removed

Grated zest and juice of 1 lemon

Kosher salt

½ cup diced celery

1 Anaheim chile, diced

2 green onions, white and green parts, thinly sliced

¼ cup finely chopped fresh flat-leaf parsley

1 clove garlic, finely grated with a zester

¼ cup extra-virgin olive oil

1 teaspoon ground guajillo chile (optional)

½ teaspoon freshly ground black pepper

Plantain chips or other crunchy chips, for serving

CEVICHE

Ceviche, a dish made of marinated raw fish, chiles, and citrus, is believed to be one of the oldest dishes in the world, with no actual recipes for its earliest incarnations. Archaeologists discovered fish and chile remains in the stomachs of mummies at one of the most ancient sites in Peru, indicating that the combination of raw fish and acid (from the chiles) dates back three thousand years. However, it wasn't until Spanish and Portuguese traders brought lemon and lime from Asia that citrus was added to the mix. As ceviche migrated throughout South and Central America, it took on a variety of flavors and techniques from different cultures.

While traditional ceviche recipes call for mixing all the ingredients together and marinating for several hours, we prefer to take a different approach. Our secret? Marinating the seafood in a seasoned acidic brine first, then adding the herbs, vegetables, and/or fruits just before serving. This technique keeps the ingredients bright and snappy, preserving their unique textures and flavors.

FLUKE CEVICHE WITH AJÍ AMARILLO

Although rooted in traditional Peruvian flavors and techniques, this preparation is inspired by Miami's dining scene, where we first discovered ceviche prepared with ají amarillo paste. Sold in jars, this Peruvian yellow chile purée is sweet, spicy, tangy, and fruity, and it packs a punch that'll take you straight to South Beach. Also known as summer flounder, fluke has a subtle flavor and delicate texture and is a popular choice for chef-driven ceviche preparations throughout Florida. If you're unable to catch or source local fluke due to location or season, snapper, rockfish, and grouper are good substitutes.

In a bowl, combine the fish, jalapeño, garlic, lime zest and juice, ají amarillo paste, kosher salt, and ground pepper. Mix gently until the fish slices are evenly coated, then pack the mixture into a storage container small enough to ensure all the fish slices are submerged in liquid. Cover and refrigerate for at least 2 hours or up to 1 day.

Meanwhile, prep the radish, tomato, cucumber, cilantro, and green onion, mix together in a small bowl, cover, and refrigerate until needed.

To serve, taste the marinated fish for seasoning and adjust with kosher salt to your liking if necessary. Scatter the fish mixture across the bottom of a serving plate or shallow bowl, then strew the vegetable mixture over the top. Finish with a pinch or so of sea salt and a few cracks of pepper. We like to accompany this ceviche with tortilla chips for scooping, snacking, and textural contrast.

Makes 2–6 servings

8 oz fluke fillet, cut into 2-inch-wide strips, then thinly sliced

½ jalapeño chile, finely chopped

1 clove garlic, finely grated with a zester

Grated zest and juice of 1 lime

2 tablespoons ají amarillo paste

½ teaspoon kosher salt

¼ teaspoon freshly ground black pepper

¼ cup diced radish

¼ cup diced tomato

¼ cup diced English cucumber

2 tablespoons finely chopped fresh cilantro

1 green onion, white and green parts, thinly sliced

Flaky sea salt and freshly cracked black pepper, for finishing

Tortilla chips, for serving

SAVANNAH-STYLE COBIA CRUDO

Inspired by our dining experiences around Savannah, this raw-fish dish combines juicy peaches, sweet, buttery pecans, and the tangy zip of buttermilk with cobia, one of our favorite fish species. A tropical whitefish beloved by chefs and anglers alike, cobia has large, dense loins that are often grilled or roasted, yet we find the meat to be delicate enough to serve uncooked. If you're unable to catch or source local cobia due to location or season, look for Open Blue, a sustainable aquaculture operation based out of Florida with open net–pen farms in Panama. Other species that we think go great with this setup include black bass, tuna, and sea scallops.

In a bowl, combine the fish, buttermilk, lime zest and juice, and kosher salt and mix gently. Make sure all the fish strips are submerged in liquid (this may require packing the mixture into a small food storage container), then cover and refrigerate for 15 minutes. Do not exceed this time or your raw fish will begin to denature and turn into more of a ceviche.

To serve, arrange the fish pieces across a chilled serving plate and pour the buttermilk mixture evenly around the dish. Shingle pieces of peach off each piece of fish. Drizzle oil around the plate, then sprinkle the pecans, sea salt, and basil across the plate in a rustic fashion. Serve immediately.

Makes 2–4 servings

8 oz cobia fillet, cut into ¼-inch-thick strips

¼ cup buttermilk

Grated zest and juice of ½ lime

¼ teaspoon kosher salt

1 ripe peach (see Note), halved, pitted, and cut into ¼-inch-thick wedges

Extra-virgin olive oil, for drizzling

1 tablespoon finely chopped toasted pecans

Flaky sea salt, for finishing

5–7 small fresh basil leaves

Note: If peaches are not in season, substitute another stone fruit in season, such as apricots, nectarines, plums, pluots, or cherries.

GULF COAST AMBERJACK CRUDO

The greater amberjack is a prized catch throughout the South. We've even had the pleasure of landing some ourselves while fishing the coastline of Sarasota with good friend and chef Steve Phelps. Florida's culinary scene is known for its unique Floribbean cuisine, a cooking style that features ingredients and techniques from the Caribbean, Latin America, Spain, Portugal, and Africa. Here, we draw inspiration from our love of Cuban flavors, dressing the fish in a light yet lively blend of orange, lemon, and lime juices along with raw garlic. We stamped it Southern by adding collard greens and fresh horseradish root to what would have been a traditional Argentinean chimichurri.

Amberjack is a member of the Carangidae family, which includes the jacks and pompanos. The Japanese revere jacks for their firm, buttery flesh. Most quality sushi restaurants serve a variety of species from this family, including hamachi (Japanese yellowtail), kanpachi (greater amberjack), and hiramasa (yellowtail amberjack). Since jacks are commonly called yellow*tail* and served at sushi joints, they're often confused with yellow*fin* (tuna), despite being no relation. Hence, jacks are often mislabeled and misunderstood.

If you can't get your hands on local amberjack due to location or season, look for Dutch yellowtail, a sashimi-grade product that is sustainably farmed in the Netherlands.

In a bowl, combine the fish; orange, lemon, and lime zest and juice; garlic; and kosher salt and mix gently. Make sure all the fish strips are submerged in liquid (this may require packing the mixture into a small food storage container), then cover and refrigerate for 15 minutes. Do not exceed this time or your raw fish will begin to denature and turn into more of a ceviche.

To serve, arrange the pieces of fish across a chilled serving plate and pour the citrus mixture evenly around the dish. Spoon a small bit of chimichurri onto each fish strip and add a serrano slice (if using). Drizzle oil around the plate, then scatter the pickled onion, cilantro, and sea salt across the plate in a rustic fashion. Serve immediately.

Makes 2–4 servings

8 oz center-cut amberjack fillet, cut into 1/4-inch-thick strips

Grated zest and juice of 1 orange

Grated zest and juice of 1/2 lemon

Grated zest and juice of 1/2 lime

1 clove garlic, finely grated with a zester

1/4 teaspoon kosher salt

2–3 tablespoons Collard Green Chimichurri

1 serrano chile, thinly sliced (optional)

Extra-virgin olive oil, for drizzling

2–3 tablespoons Pickled Red Onion

7–9 small fresh cilantro sprigs, for finishing

Flaky sea salt, for finishing

Collard Green Chimichurri
Makes about 2 cups

2 collard green leaves, stemmed and roughly chopped
1 cup roughly chopped fresh cilantro
2 cloves garlic, roughly chopped
2 green onions, white and green parts, roughly chopped
1 serrano chile, roughly chopped (optional)
2 tablespoons peeled and grated fresh horseradish root, or 1 tablespoon prepared horseradish
Grated zest and juice of 1 lemon
½ teaspoon kosher salt
½ cup extra-virgin olive oil

In a food processor, combine the collard leaves, cilantro, garlic, green onions, chile (if using), horseradish, lemon zest and juice, and salt and pulse until finely chopped. Pour into a bowl, add the oil, and stir together gently. Taste for seasoning and adjust with salt to your liking if necessary.

Use right away, or transfer to an airtight container and refrigerate for up to 1 week, then bring to room temperature before using.

. . .

Pickled Red Onion
Makes about ½ cup

½ red onion, thinly sliced
Grated zest and juice of 1 lime
½ teaspoon kosher salt

In a bowl, combine the onion, lime zest and juice, and salt and mix thoroughly with your hands, massaging the lime juice into the onion. Pack into an airtight container, making sure the onion slices are submerged in the lime juice, and let sit for at least 1 hour before using. The pickled onion will keep in the refrigerator for up to 1 month.

Finishing with Sea Salt

Sea salt is harvested directly from seawater and contains a variety of minerals that impart a more complex taste and texture than salt made from sedimentary deposits. Good sea salt can be pricey, but a little goes a long way, and it's worth the investment to elevate your dishes.

One fascinating aspect of sea salt is the concept of terroir, which refers to the unique environmental factors that affect the taste of a particular food or drink. In the same way that wine grapes can express the soil and climate of a region, a sea salt can reflect the nutrients, algae, and other factors present in the waters where it was harvested.

By using sea salt to finish a dish, you can taste the essence of the coastal community from which it was harvested. For instance, by finishing a snapper freshly caught off the coast of North Carolina with sea salt produced in the state, you create a beautiful harmony in the dish that transports you to those Carolinian shores. It's a simple yet powerful way to connect to a region's culinary culture and heritage.

KEY WEST PINK SHRIMP AGUACHILE

The influence of Mexican flavors on Southern cuisine is undeniable, and this dish is a celebration of these rich culinary traditions coming together in one mouthwatering bite. Aguachile, literally "chile water," is a close cousin of ceviche that has evolved to become a shrimp-focused specialty. We find Key West pink shrimp to be an impeccable fit here, as they are bite size and their plump, sweet meat is delightfully complemented by the refreshing nature of aguachile. If you can't source Key West pink shrimp, look for other regionally wild-caught shrimp in the 31/40-count range, be they brown or white.

In a saucepan over high heat, bring the water to a rolling boil and salt the water lightly with kosher salt. Add the shrimp, reduce the heat to maintain a gentle simmer, and cook the shrimp until they are about 85 percent done, about 1½ minutes.

Immediately drain the shrimp into a colander and then lay them in a single layer on a sheet pan. Do not rinse the shrimp or shock them in an ice bath. This is a common mistake that causes a major loss of flavor. The shrimp will finish cooking in the residual heat and in the acid in the marinade. Slip the sheet pan into the refrigerator until the shrimp are well chilled, about 1 hour.

While the shrimp are chilling, prepare the aguachile sauce. Authentic aguachile always has a touch of heat, hence the addition of the jalapeño. This recipe yields a mild heat level. To bump up the heat, add the optional serrano, and if you crave a delightfully spicy dish, add the habanero too.

To make the sauce, set aside ½ cup of the cilantro for garnish and add the remainder to a blender along with the cucumber, jalapeño, serrano and habanero (if using), garlic, lime zest and juice, and ½ teaspoon kosher salt and blend on high speed until you have a deep green sauce, about 1 minute.

When the shrimp are well chilled, transfer them to a bowl, add the sauce, and mix well. Pack into an airtight container and refrigerate for at least overnight or up to 3 days.

To serve, pour the shrimp and sauce into a serving bowl. Scatter the sliced avocado, radish, and reserved cilantro over the top. Finish with some sea salt and pepper.

Makes 2–6 servings

8 cups water

Kosher salt

1 lb large Key West pink shrimp (31/40), peeled and deveined

1 bunch fresh cilantro, roughly chopped

½ English cucumber, peeled and diced

1 jalapeño chile, diced

1 serrano chile, diced (optional)

1 habanero chile, diced (optional)

1 clove garlic

Grated zest and juice of 1 lime

½ avocado, peeled and thinly sliced, for garnish

1 radish, shaved, for garnish

Flaky sea salt and freshly cracked black pepper, for finishing

Tortilla chips or corn nuts, for serving

When we are being traditional, we serve this dish family-style and accompany it with our favorite tortilla chips. The crisp texture and masa flavor of the chips are critical components to enjoying the aguachile properly. With that said, if we're serving this dish as more of a light appetizer to be eaten with a fork rather than hands, we like to sprinkle on some corn nuts or quicos (giant Spanish corn nuts) to get that crunchy corn crackle.

CHIP SHOP SCALLOPED POTATOES

These battered and fried potatoes, which are in the style of British fish-and-chips shops, are insanely delicious with caviar. They are best when eaten immediately after they emerge from the hot oil, so we like to have everything else involved with our caviar service ready before we begin the final frying. If you don't feel like frying, you can grab some blini or toast points at most shops that offer a fine selection of caviar.

Pour oil to a depth of 4 inches into a deep, heavy pot or deep fryer and heat to 300°F. Set a wire rack on a sheet pan and place it near the stove.

When the oil is ready, add the potatoes and blanch them until just cooked through, about 3 minutes. They will not color. Using a spider or slotted spoon, transfer them to the wire rack in a single layer to drain. Let rest for 15 minutes. This blanching step is the secret to crispy, creamy potatoes.

Line a plate with paper towels and place it near the stove. Increase the oil temperature to 350°F. Working in batches to avoid crowding, dip the potato slices in the batter, allowing the excess to drip off, and then carefully slip them into the oil. Fry, flipping each potato slice halfway through cooking, until the slices are deep golden brown, 3–4 minutes. Using the spider or spoon, transfer the slices to the towel-lined plate. Lightly season immediately with salt. Repeat until all the slices are battered and fried. Serve piping hot with caviar, if using.

Makes 2–4 servings

3–4 quarts oil, for deep-frying

1–2 large Yukon Gold potatoes, peeled and cut crosswise into ¼-inch-thick slices

Light & Crispy Beer Batter (page 149)

Kosher salt

Caviar, for serving (optional)

PROPER CAVIAR SERVICE

Indulging in caviar need not be an elitist affair, as there are various delicious fish roes available at an affordable price. We believe that the charm of enjoying caviar lies in the interactive experience of savoring small, salty bites of elegance with loved ones.

While there are traditional protocols for presenting caviar, you can have fun with it and create your own unique aesthetic. In our own presentations, we like to use an eclectic assortment of small bowls and spoons. Stemming from an era when only the rich ate caviar (and the rich only ate with sterling silver flatware), there is a lot of misinformation out there about spoons and caviar. As a metal, silver can react with caviar and cause a metallic, bitter taste. However, other metals, such as stainless steel, do not. The variety of materials we find to be both elegant and safe for caviar service include mother-of-pearl, animal horn, wood, ceramic, and stainless steel.

The essential aspects of properly presenting caviar involve serving it in its tin over crushed ice and surrounding it with a variety of traditional accompaniments, including crème fraîche, chives, red onion, hard-boiled eggs (yolks and whites separated), and either blini or toast points. For crushing ice, we recommend using a Lewis bag and an ice mallet (heavy canvas bag and wooden mallet found in every cocktail bar). But if you don't have either handy, a tea towel and the base of a heavy saucepan will suffice.

Our go-to caviar choices are bowfin, hackleback, lumpfish, paddlefish, sturgeon, and trout. Our top three favorite caviars produced sustainably in the US are Smoked Rainbow Trout caviar from Sunburst Trout Farms, Black American Bowfin caviar (Cajun name "Choupique caviar") from Marky's, and the creme de la creme—Royal Sturgeon caviar from Sterling.

CAROLINA-STYLE COLOSSAL SHRIMP COCKTAIL

Nothing screams Southern summer like a platter of chilled shrimp cocktail. This preparation is all about simplicity, technique, and letting the quality of the shellfish shine. The coastal South is home to some of the world's finest wild-caught shrimp, offering three species to choose from for this recipe: white, brown, and pink. Due to the overlapping seasonality of these species, there's a good chance you will find market-fresh shrimp any time of year. However, shrimp freezes and thaws extremely well, so don't hesitate to purchase frozen.

In a large stockpot over high heat, combine the water and 1 tablespoon of the seasoning and bring to a rolling boil. Add the shrimp, reduce the heat to maintain a gentle simmer, and cook until just done, about 3 minutes.

Immediately drain the shrimp into a colander and transfer to a bowl. Do not rinse the shrimp or shock them in an ice bath. This is a common mistake that causes a major loss of flavor. Add the remaining 1 tablespoon seasoning to the shrimp and toss to coat evenly, then lay the shrimp in a single layer on a sheet pan. Slip the sheet pan into the refrigerator until the shrimp are well chilled, about 1 hour.

Transfer the shrimp to a bowl, add the lemon zest and juice, and mix well. Pack into an airtight container and refrigerate for at least overnight or up to 3 days.

Serve the shrimp well chilled—on ice if you like—with the rémoulade for dipping and dunking.

Makes 4–8 servings

5 quarts water

2 tablespoons Lowcountry Boil Seasoning (page 239) or Old Bay Seasoning

2 lb wild-caught Atlantic or Gulf super colossal shrimp (U12), peeled and deveined

Grated zest and juice of 1/2 lemon

Red Rémoulade (page 243) or Chunky Creole Cocktail Sauce (page 244), for serving

CAJUN LOBSTER COCKTAIL

If you think lobster is just a New England specialty, think again. We've put our own spin on this beloved crustacean, and it's bold, spicy, and oh so Southern. Instead of the usual lemon and tartar, we go for a zingy lime and Cajun seasoning combo, which we recommend be enjoyed with plenty of red hot and rémoulade. Our recipe calls for Caribbean spiny lobster, as it is a native species of the waters of the coastal South. Although these lobsters don't have large, meat-packed claws, they do boast a sweet, meaty tail, making them the true king of cocktail shellfish. If you're unable to find them, you can substitute the better-known American lobster, which makes its way down south as far as Cape Hatteras, North Carolina.

In a large stockpot over high heat, combine the water and 1 tablespoon of the seasoning and bring to a rolling boil. Add the lobster tails, reduce the heat to maintain a gentle simmer, and cook until *just* done, about 3 minutes.

Immediately drain the lobster tails into a colander and transfer to a bowl. Do not rinse the lobster tails or shock them in an ice bath. This is a common mistake that causes a major loss of flavor. Add the remaining 1 tablespoon seasoning to the lobster tails and toss to coat evenly, then lay the lobster tails in a single layer on a sheet pan. Slip the sheet pan into the refrigerator until the lobster tails are well chilled, about 1 hour.

Transfer the lobster tails to a bowl, add the lime zest and juice, and mix well. Pack into an airtight container and refrigerate for at least overnight or up to 3 days.

Serve the lobster tails well chilled—on ice if you like—with the rémoulade for dipping and dunking.

Makes 4–6 servings

5 quarts water

2 tablespoons Cajun seasoning, homemade (page 240) or store-bought

6 Caribbean spiny lobster tails, 8 oz each, halved lengthwise

Grated zest and juice of 1 lime

2 tablespoons chopped fresh flat-leaf parsley

1 green onion, white and green parts, thinly sliced

Miso Lime Rémoulade (page 244), Chunky Creole Cocktail Sauce (page 244), Sea Salt–Fermented Red Hot Sauce (page 247), or other favorite condiment, for serving

NUOC CHAM CRAB SALAD

As you make your way along the Gulf Coast of Texas, the vibrant Vietnamese influence is hard to miss. Despite a rocky start with the arrival of the first wave of refugees after the Fall of Saigon in 1975, Vietnamese culture, particularly the cuisine, has been woven into the fabric of the Lone Star State.

Nuoc cham is an extremely dynamic Vietnamese cold sauce that can be used for dipping or dressing. It is revered as one of the great condiments of the world and is an absolute flavor bomb, boasting a pungent explosion of umami, sweetness, saltiness, and sourness. We find these flavors to be fantastic for dressing a crab salad, especially one packed with loads of upbeat herbs. You can pile the salad into lettuce cups or avocado halves, serve it in a toasted buttery brioche roll with mayo and shredded lettuce, or simply accompany it with crackers. If you end up with leftovers, this salad makes a great base for a bowl of pad Thai. Just add rice noodles, scrambled eggs, and peanuts.

In a bowl, combine the crabmeat, cilantro, mint, basil, chile (if using), garlic, fish sauce, chile garlic sauce (if using), sugar, lime zest and juice, and salt. Gently fold together all the ingredients until well mixed, being mindful to keep the crab chunky.

The salad can be served right away, or it can be transferred to an airtight container and refrigerated for up to 5 days.

Makes 2–4 servings

8 oz pasteurized lump or jumbo lump blue crabmeat, picked over for shell fragments

1/2 cup roughly chopped fresh cilantro

1/4 cup roughly chopped fresh mint

1/4 cup roughly chopped fresh Thai basil

1 jalapeño chile, finely chopped (optional)

1 clove garlic, finely grated with a zester

2 tablespoons fish sauce (preferably Red Boat)

1 teaspoon chile garlic sauce (optional)

1 1/2 tablespoons organic sugar

Grated zest and juice of 1 lime

1/2 teaspoon kosher salt

YELLOWFIN TUNA & WATERMELON SALAD

For this recipe, we've paired succulent yellowfin tuna with juicy watermelon, creating a vibrant and refreshing salad that's perfect for a hot summer day. The sweetness of the watermelon perfectly complements the rich flavor of the tuna, while the fresh herbs and coconut bring everything together in a symphony of flavors.

Yellowfin is a sustainable red-meat tuna that's celebrated for its richness and versatility, as it can be enjoyed in a great variety of preparations, both raw and cooked. We love the tangy tack of its flesh and always light up when we come across locally landed loins.

Tuna are fast, migratory species that travel the world's oceans. They're top predators in the marine food chain and provide an important balance throughout the ocean environment. These magnificent animals are prized by many global cuisines and consequently are subject to illegal and unsustainable fishing practices. Atlantic bluefin tuna have been increasingly overfished for the past decade and are currently an endangered species. Pacific bluefin are also considered vulnerable. The truth is, we shouldn't be fishing any bluefin until global populations are able to recuperate and thrive. That's a basic principle of sustainable, science-based fisheries management, so keep that in mind the next time you see bluefin tuna on a menu. As our good friend and chef William Dissen likes to say, "You wouldn't eat panda, would you?"

In a large bowl, combine the tuna, watermelon, cucumber, avocado, cilantro, basil, mint, lime zest and juice, kosher salt, and oil. Gently fold together all the ingredients until well mixed. Cover the bowl and slip it into the refrigerator until the salad is well chilled, about 1 hour.

Serve in small-to-medium individual bowls. Finish each serving with a sprinkling of the coconut and sea salt.

Makes 2–4 servings

8 oz fresh (never frozen) yellowfin tuna fillet, diced

2 cups peeled and diced seedless watermelon

1 cup diced English cucumber

1 avocado, halved, pitted, peeled, and diced

½ cup roughly chopped fresh cilantro

½ cup roughly chopped fresh basil

¼ cup roughly chopped fresh mint

Grated zest and juice of 1 lime

½ teaspoon kosher salt

2 tablespoons toasted sesame oil

2 tablespoons unsweetened dried coconut flakes, toasted

Flaky sea salt, for finishing

Why We Avoid Bright Red Tuna

Elevating your culinary experience begins with selecting high-quality ingredients. When it comes to tuna, many people have been deceived by the allure of bright red flesh, only to be disappointed by its lackluster taste and soggy texture.

This disappointment is often due to the use of carbon monoxide, an FDA-approved but EU-, Japan-, and Canada-banned process. While it enhances the fish's appearance, it conceals its true freshness and flavor. Authentic tuna displays deep crimson red, purple, or even brown hues, offering a unique texture and a rich, tangy umami profile.

For those seeking sustainable choices, Seafood Watch offers valuable guidance. It's important to note that you can find sustainably caught tuna that has undergone the gassing process, underlining the complexities of sourcing seafood in today's global marketplace. Certifying bodies, like Seafood Watch, focus on responsible sourcing but may not cover essential post-harvest factors such as processing, packaging, labeling, and shipping.

By delving into the intricacies of the global seafood industry, we can all become more discerning consumers, enrich our cooking, and actively contribute to the promotion of healthier oceans.

ON OYSTERS

The oyster is a delicacy valued around the world, and nowhere is this more evident than in the coastal South. While oysters can be prepared in countless ways, nothing quite compares to expertly shucked oysters on the half shell served up on a bed of crushed ice. But in order to truly appreciate this iconic dish, it is important to understand the fundamentals of sourcing, preparing, and serving.

The Iconic Oyster

Raw oysters are a cultural phenomenon, enjoyed by locals and tourists alike. Any notable oyster house will have a system in place that allows even the most inexperienced oyster lover to indulge in an assortment of types accompanied by tasting notes. Oysters are not only delicious but are also one of the cleanest and healthiest marine foods. They filter out pollutants, leaving behind cleaner water, and raising them as part of a holistic land and water management system offers a natural aid to our polluted food system. In fact, one oyster can filter up to fifty gallons of water each day.

Aquaculture Done Right

One of the many benefits of farming oysters is the mollusks' ability to remove excess nitrogen, a by-product of industrial agriculture, from our waters. Although nitrogen is a natural nutrient of aquatic ecosystems, too much of it degrades water quality and food sources, making it the worst ocean pollutant. This does not mean that the oyster itself becomes polluted or toxic. It is instead a great example of how the earth and our oceans have their own natural system of checks and balances. So when our good friend and farmer Lane Zirlott, of Murder Point Oysters in Alabama, plants thirty million oysters, his farming operation has a significant impact on cleansing the Gulf. And that's why almost all oysters we eat are sustainably farmed.

The Important Role of Sustainable Aquaculture

Aquaculture is the fastest-growing food system on the planet, and with the implementation of innovation and social equity, it is quickly becoming our most sustainable one as well. As we move toward the year 2050, when there will be roughly ten billion people on the planet, sustainable aquaculture presents a multitude of solutions for achieving a healthier, more bountiful food system. To better understand the future of food sourcing, we urge you to reevaluate what you think you know about farm-raised seafood. Ask yourself why we celebrate terrestrial sustainable farmers but not those of the marine environment. It is imperative that we shift our paradigm on the production of aquatic organisms in controlled environments and increase the global market demand for the adoption of sustainable aquaculture practices.

Southern Oyster Farms

Currently, the southeastern Atlantic and Gulf coasts are home to some of the finest and most sustainable oyster farms in the world. From North Carolina down the Atlantic and throughout the Gulf Coast, here are our twenty favorite Southern oysters:

Hatteras Salts—Cape Hatteras Oyster Co. (Buxton, NC), Fat Bellies—Crystal Coast Oysters (Morehead City, NC), Dukes of Topsail Sound—N Sea Oyster Co. (Hampstead, NC), Beau Sels—Oysters Carolina (Harkers Island, NC), Lowcountry Cups—Lowcountry Oyster Co. (Green Pond, SC), Sea Clouds—Barrier Island Oyster Co. (Charleston, SC),

Single Ladies—Lady's Island Oyster (Beaufort, SC), Steamboat Creek Oyster Farm (Edisto Island, SC), E.L. McIntosh & Son Oyster Co. (Harris Neck, GA), Little Honeys—Cypress Point Oysters (Spring Creek, FL), Salty Birds—Pelican Oyster Co. (Tallahassee, FL), Saucey Lady Oyster Co. (Panacea, FL), Murder Point Oysters (Bayou La Batre, AL), Point aux Pins (Bayou La Batre, AL), Isle Dauphines—Mobile Oyster Co. (Dauphin Island, AL), Admiral Shellfish Co. (Fort Morgan, AL), French Hermit Oyster Co. (Deer Island, MS), Rosa Golds—Bayou Rosa Oyster Farm (Lafourche Parish, LA), Bright Side Oysters (Grand Isle, LA), Southern Belles—Grand Isle Sea Farms (Grand Isle, LA)

Sourcing

When sourcing oysters, look for a local seafood counter that offers in-shell oysters stored on ice. If purveyors sell oysters year-round, there's a good chance they have a passion for them and know what they're doing. To ensure freshness, ask to see the shellstock tag. The law requires that all fresh, raw, in-shell molluscan

shellfish be packed with a shellstock tag, which must be kept on file for ninety days. The tag will show you the date and location of the harvest, which should clear up any concerns you may have.

Oysters can remain fresh and alive for up to two weeks when stored under proper refrigeration, but we recommend buying them no more than two days in advance of serving. Most good seafood purveyors will pack your oysters in a bag of crushed ice, but if they don't, request it. The bag should not be sealed, or the oysters will suffocate and die.

Scrubbing and Storing

Scrub your oysters as soon as you get them into your kitchen. To properly clean oysters, scrub both sides of the exterior shell with a natural-fiber brush or a shellfish-specific scrubbing tool to remove any brittle shell fragments or organic residue that has formed throughout the oyster's life. Keep two piles of oysters on ice: those you haven't yet scrubbed and those you have, with your sink in the middle. Run cold water onto the oyster while scrubbing, and scrub the oysters quickly to ensure they stay ice-cold. Place the cleaned oysters evenly on a tray or in a shallow pan and put the tray or pan in the back of the refrigerator, toward the bottom, where it's often coldest.

Shucking and Serving

Shucking oysters can be intimidating, but anyone can get good at it quickly with the right system, technique, and tools. You'll need plenty of ice, clean kitchen towels, and a proper shucker.

As for the shucker, we have a few tried-and-true recommendations. Toadfish, a Charleston-based coastal lifestyle company that replants and replenishes oyster habitats, produces the top two reasonably priced oyster shuckers on the market, the Toadfish Professional Edition oyster knife (white handle) and the Put 'Em Back oyster knife (blue handle). Both shuckers have a unique design and are comfortable to hold, and the price point makes them the best widely

available options. For those seeking a more elevated, handmade, and artisanal shucker, the Brew shucker by Middleton Made Knives, which features an AEB-L stainless-steel blade with a built-in bottle opener and a DymaLux handle, is a beautiful and durable choice.

Before shucking, set up your station with in-shell oysters on ice to your left, a sturdy cutting board with a damp towel in front of you, and a pan of fresh ice to your right for landing shucked oysters. Have kitchen towels, trifolded lengthwise, directly in front of your cutting board. We prefer a fresh towel for every two dozen oysters to keep the process as clean as possible.

To shuck an oyster, position the oyster cupped shell side down on the towel, with the hinge pointing toward you, and hold it firmly in place with the towel in your nondominant hand. Using your dominant hand, insert the tip of your shucking tool into the hinge at a 45- to 90-degree angle, then apply gentle pressure and a back-and-forth twisting motion until you feel a pop. Rotate your tool and slide it across the top shell to

separate the abductor muscle, then lift off the top shell. Now scrape the blade along the bottom shell in one motion to sever the other side of the abductor muscle while flipping the oyster. Place the shucked oyster, still on its bottom shell, on ice and repeat. Keep your shucker, towel, and hands clean to avoid shell fragments. It may seem intimidating at first, but after shucking a few dozen oysters, you'll be a pro.

Serve your oysters on a bed of crushed ice (serving oysters on salt doesn't offer any value). We use a Lewis bag and a mallet (sturdy canvas bag and wooden mallet indispensable to bartenders) to crush the ice, but a kitchen towel and a heavy saucepan will do the trick. Offer whatever accoutrements you like (see Salinity, following), such as hot sauce, mignonette, lemon wedges, cocktail sauce, and/or saltines. Check out our Sundries chapter (page 229) if you'd like to craft your own accompaniments.

Salinity

To best pair accoutrements with your oysters, it's helpful to know their salinity level, measured in parts per thousand (PPT). Below 12 PPT is low salinity, 12–20 PPT is medium, and 20+ PPT is rich and briny. Higher-salinity oysters can handle bolder condiments, like hot sauce and cocktail sauce, while lower-salinity ones are best enjoyed as is or with something simple, such as mignonette or lemon. Saltines offer a textural contrast and are an old-school accompaniment. You can typically locate the salinity specifics of your oysters either through the farm's website or by scanning the QR code located on the shellstock tag.

Oyster South

For more information on the beloved oyster, check out our friends over at Oyster South—a nonprofit organization that connects communities and provides resources to foster the success of oyster farming in the South. They do great work throughout the oyster-farming industry, connecting chefs, shuckers, and seafood dealers to oyster lovers everywhere. They have a ton of resources available on their website (oystersouth.com), including links to purchase almost five dozen different oyster varieties direct from their respective farms. Oyster South also offers a variety of memberships and events, with an epic annual symposium that is quite possibly the greatest oyster-focused event in the world. Seriously.

PINCHOS

WE BELIEVE THE BEST WAY TO EXPERIENCE A new place is through its food. From breakfast at a cozy café to happy-hour bites and appetizers, we love to indulge in the flavors of different cultures. Pinchos is a Basque term that means "thorns" or "spikes," and refers to small snacks that are skewered with tooth-picks. Although *pinchos* are a category of Spanish tapas, to us, they represent the merriment of togetherness and exploration through bite-size foods for the table. The recipes in this chapter feature a playfully delicious mash-up of coastal cuisines of the South and beyond, served in small bites that will leave your taste buds wanting more. We invite y'all to whip up your own unique spread and savor the flavors of our global culinary adventures.

JAMAICAN JERK CONCH FRITTERS

Get ready for an absolute explosion of flavor. While Jamaican fritters traditionally feature salt fish, and conch fritters are most commonly found in the Bahamas and Key West, we've decided to mix things up and combine the two for a taste sensation you won't soon forget. The real magic lies in the jerk seasoning, which we believe is one of the best seasonings for fried foods. It's even delicious on French fries dipped in mango ketchup, but we digress. We've paired our fritters with our zesty ginger lemongrass rémoulade that perfectly complements the big flavors of the seasoning and adds an extra layer of aromatic goodness.

There are a few options for getting your hands on conch or clams for this preparation. You'll often find these products already chopped and either frozen or tinned. Your best bet for acquiring conch is to check out a local Latin market or to order online. Our fail-safe here is to grab a can of Bar Harbor chopped clams. They're delicious, sweet, and stocked by a variety of national grocers.

Pour oil to a depth of 4 inches into a deep fryer or deep, heavy pot and heat to 350°F.

While the oil heats, in a food processor, combine the conch, eggs, celery, onion, Anaheim chile, and Scotch bonnet (if using), and pulse until finely chopped but still somewhat chunky. Pour the mixture into a bowl, add the flour, baking powder, salt, and jerk seasoning, and fold together with a rubber spatula until well mixed. (The fritter batter can be made in advance and stored in the refrigerator for up to 5 days.)

When the oil is ready, using a medium-size cookie scoop (about 1 1/2 tablespoons) or by eye with a spoon, scoop the batter and carefully drop it into the hot oil. Fry the fritters in batches of 8–10 until deep golden brown and cooked through, about 4 minutes. Using a spider or a slotted spoon, transfer the fritters to a bowl and immediately season with salt and jerk seasoning. Repeat until all the batter is cooked.

Serve the fritters hot with the rémoulade and hot sauce.

Makes 16–20 fritters

Neutral oil, for deep-frying

1 cup roughly chopped conch or clams

2 large eggs

1 celery rib, roughly chopped

1/2 yellow onion, roughly chopped

1 Anaheim chile, roughly chopped

1 Scotch bonnet or habanero chile, roughly chopped (optional)

2 cups all-purpose flour

1 tablespoon baking powder

2 teaspoons kosher salt, plus more for sprinkling

2 teaspoons Jamaican Jerk Seasoning (page 240), plus more for sprinkling

Ginger Lemongrass Rémoulade (page 244) and Funky Tropical Hot Sauce (page 246), for serving

LOUISIANA CRAWFISH HUSHPUPPIES

When it comes to fritters, every corner of the globe seems to have its own unique spin, from India's pakoras to Italy's arancini to France's beloved beignets. But for us Southerners, there's nothing quite like a good hushpuppy. One thing that's so great about hushpuppies is that they're endlessly adaptable. Whether you prefer them round and smooth or rustic and finger shaped, dry and cornmeal heavy or moist with wheat flour, you can be sure there's a hushpuppy out there for you. Our version keeps things classic but with a twist that'll transport your taste buds straight to Louisiana. By infusing the "holy trinity" of celery, green pepper, and onion into the mix, we've created a fritter that practically begs to be paired with succulent crawfish. We like serving the hushpuppies with our green chile flavored butter, but your favorite hot sauce would also be good.

Pour oil to a depth of 4 inches into a deep fryer or deep, heavy pot and heat to 350°F. Lay a brown paper bag on a sheet pan (or line the pan with paper towels) and set it near the stove.

While the oil heats, in a large bowl, whisk together the flour, cornmeal, baking powder, and seasoning. In a small bowl, whisk together the buttermilk and egg until blended. In a food processor, combine the onion, chile, and garlic and purée until smooth.

Add the vegetable purée to the buttermilk mixture and whisk until incorporated. Pour the wet ingredients into the flour mixture and mix with a rubber spatula until evenly moistened. Add the crawfish and fold in until well incorporated. Have ready another, unlined sheet pan. Using a scoop or spoon, form balls of the mixture about 1½ inches in diameter, lining them up in rows on the unlined pan.

When the oil is ready, working in batches to avoid crowding, carefully place 6–8 balls into the hot oil and fry until deep golden brown, about 3 minutes. Using a spider or a slotted spoon, transfer the hushpuppies to the lined sheet pan to absorb excess oil. Sprinkle immediately with a little seasoning. Repeat until all the balls are fried.

Let the hushpuppies rest for a few minutes before enjoying them with plenty of green chile butter for dipping.

Makes 18–22 hushpuppies

Neutral oil, for deep-frying

1 cup all-purpose flour

2/3 cup cornmeal

1 tablespoon baking powder

1 tablespoon Lowcountry Boil Seasoning (page 239) or Old Bay Seasoning, plus more for sprinkling

½ cup buttermilk

1 large egg

¼ red onion, roughly chopped

1 poblano chile, roughly chopped

4 cloves garlic

1 lb frozen Louisiana crawfish tail meat, thawed, rinsed, and drained

Whipped Green Chile Butter, for serving

Whipped Green Chile Butter
Makes about 2 cups

1 can (4 oz) fire-roasted diced green chiles, drained
1 cup (8 oz) salted butter, at room temperature

In a stand mixer fitted with the paddle attachment, combine the diced green chiles and butter and beat on medium speed until well mixed. Increase the speed to medium-high and continue to beat until the color lightens and the texture is fluffy, 3–4 minutes.

Use right away or keep in an airtight container in the refrigerator for up to 2 weeks. Serve at room temperature.

CATFISH & COUNTRY HAM CROQUETAS

Indulge in the crispy and creamy goodness of croquetas with a Southern twist. These thumb-size delicacies are a specialty of the Catalonian kitchen, but we've given them a touch of coastal Southern flavor with the addition of catfish and country ham. While the traditional croquetas de jamón and croquetas de bacalao are indeed iconic, these catfish and ham croquetas are serious competition. There are a whole bunch of dipping sauces that go great with them, but we have found our spicy Calabrian Chile Rémoulade to be the perfect flavor bridge between the US South and Southern Europe.

In a large skillet over medium heat, sweat the butter and ham until the ham pieces start to render their fat and curl around the edges, 2–3 minutes. Add the catfish, season lightly with salt and pepper, and cook, stirring somewhat frequently, until the fish is cooked, 5–7 minutes. Add the water, bring to a simmer, and then add the instant potatoes. Cook, stirring frequently, until the potatoes have rehydrated and absorbed all the moisture, 1–2 minutes.

Transfer the mixture to a food processor and purée until well mixed and as smooth as possible, 1–2 minutes. The catfish and ham will not purée to a completely smooth consistency, but some texture here is welcome. Transfer the mixture to a bowl, cover, and refrigerate until fully chilled, about 30 minutes.

Just before the mixture has finished chilling, pour oil to a depth of 4 inches into a deep fryer or deep, heavy pot and heat to 350°F. Lay a brown paper bag on a sheet pan (or line the pan with paper towels) and set it near the stove.

Have ready another, unlined sheet pan. Add the egg to the chilled mixture and mix until fully incorporated. Using your hands, scoop up and shape the mixture into cylinders roughly 2 inches long and 1 inch thick, placing them on the unlined pan as they are ready. Keep your hands clean by dipping them into cold water after shaping every few croquetas. This will help prevent the mixture from sticking to your hands and make the shaping process much easier.

Makes 15–18 croquetas

2 tablespoons salted butter

2 oz country ham, diced

8 oz catfish fillet, diced

Kosher salt and freshly ground black pepper

3/4 cup water

3/4 cup instant mashed potatoes

1 large egg

Neutral oil, for deep-frying

Panko Crunch (page 150)

Calabrian Chile Rémoulade (page 244), for serving

Following the directions for Panko Crunch, bread the croquetas, placing them on a wire rack set on a sheet pan or directly on another sheet pan.

When the oil is ready, working in batches of 5–6 croquetas, gently slip the croquetas into the hot oil and fry until deep golden brown and cooked through, about 4 minutes. Using a spider or a slotted spoon, transfer the croquetas to the lined sheet pan to absorb excess oil and lightly season immediately with salt and pepper. Repeat until all the croquetas are cooked.

Serve the croquetas hot with the rémoulade.

CRAB & GREEN CHILE PIMENTO CHEESE

Food is more than just fuel for the body. It's a symbol of our identity and history, and pimento cheese is a shining example of that. From family gatherings to tailgate parties, this spread is a staple of Southern hospitality that has made its way into the hearts and stomachs of many. But did y'all know that the original recipe didn't even come from the South? That's right, historians trace the roots of pimento cheese to the North. But it was Southerners who took commercially produced versions and made them their own with homemade recipes and such local ingredients as Georgia-grown pimentos. Nowadays, every cook has a special recipe for pimento cheese, but there's one ingredient that reigns supreme: Duke's mayo. We're not ones to mess with tradition, but we do like to add a little twist to our pimento cheese by tossing in some fresh crabmeat, green chiles, and a dash of green hot sauce for extra zing.

In a bowl, combine the crabmeat, chiles, both cheeses, mayonnaise, hot sauce, and pepper and gently fold together with a rubber spatula or wooden spoon until well mixed. Cover and refrigerate until well chilled before serving.

Serve the chilled pimento cheese with plenty of crackers. We prefer an assortment of Ritz for a classic "grandmother's house" vibe.

Makes 2 cups

8 oz pasteurized blue crab claw meat, picked over for shell fragments

1 can (4 oz) mild or hot diced green chiles, drained

4 oz Colby-Jack cheese, grated

4 oz sharp yellow Cheddar cheese, grated

⅓ cup Duke's mayonnaise

2 tablespoons Bourbon Barrel–Aged Green Hot Sauce (page 246) or green Tabasco sauce

¼ teaspoon freshly ground black pepper

Crackers, such as Ritz, for serving

PEANUT CHILE CRISP– BUTTER SHRIMP

This recipe proves that sometimes the simplest ingredients can make for the most memorable flavors. With just shrimp, chile crisp, butter, cilantro, lime zest, and salt, this dish packs a punch. Inspired by the classic Spanish dish gambas al ajillo, the flavors are a harmonious balance of spicy and buttery with a hint of citrus. Staples in most Southern and Asian kitchens, the peanuts add a rich depth to this dish. These shrimp are quick and easy to make and are best enjoyed in the traditional pinchos manner, skewered with toothpicks. Whenever possible, we use shrimp from Florida-based Sun Shrimp (page 88) for making this dish.

Preheat a large cast-iron skillet, Dutch oven, or sauté pan over medium heat for 3 minutes. Add the butter, chile crisp, and shrimp and stir until well mixed. Lightly season with salt and cook, stirring somewhat frequently, until the shrimp are cooked, 3–5 minutes.

Remove from the heat and fold in the cilantro. Spoon into a cazuela, cocotte, or serving bowl, grate the zest of the lime directly over the dish, and serve. These shrimp are delightful as is, but sometimes we like to enjoy them with crusty bread for dipping.

Makes 2–6 servings

4 tablespoons salted butter

¼ cup Peanut Chile Crisp or a mix of store-bought chile crisp and finely chopped peanuts

1 lb large shrimp (preferably from Sun Shrimp), peeled and deveined

Kosher salt

½ cup finely chopped fresh cilantro

1 lime

Crusty bread slices, for serving (optional)

. . .

Peanut Chile Crisp
Makes 3 cups

1 cup unsalted roasted peanuts

1 cup Korean chile flakes (gochugaru)

1 tablespoon firmly packed organic dark brown sugar

1 tablespoon granulated garlic

1 teaspoon kosher salt

½ cup avocado or canola oil

¼ cup toasted sesame oil

In a food processor, combine the peanuts, chile flakes, sugar, garlic, and salt and pulse until finely chopped, about 30 seconds. Add both oils and process until well incorporated, about 30 seconds.

Use right away, or pack into an airtight container and store in a cool, dark cupboard for up to 3 months. The chile crisp is best when enjoyed at room temperature or in a cooked dish.

SUN SHRIMP

Nestled in the quaint town of Pine Island, Florida, Sun Shrimp boasts a farm-to-table experience like no other. With a fully integrated on-land farm, Sun Shrimp handles every step of the process, from mating to shipping, resulting in some of the most sustainably sourced shrimp available.

But what truly sets Sun Shrimp apart is its commitment to innovation. It is equipped with a state-of-the-art DNA lab where scientists track the genetic traits of the shrimp and use that data to breed the best-tasting, non-GMO shrimp possible. And boy, can you taste the difference! These plump, juicy, sweet shrimp have just the right amount of snap to take your seafood game to the next level.

What's more, Sun Shrimp's hatchlings are in such high demand that they're even shipped to farms all across the globe. From its pristine waters to your plate, Sun Shrimp is a testament to the deliciousness and sustainability of aquaculture that can be achieved when passion meets innovation.

MARINATED MUSSELS TOAST

In the South, we take our carbs seriously, and there's no better way to indulge in a loaf of bread than with some juicy tomatoes and a touch of garlic. That's why we can't get enough of the Spanish classic pan con tomate. Made with just crusty bread, heirloom tomatoes, and a drizzle of olive oil, it's a simple dish that never disappoints. But why stop there? We've taken this traditional preparation to the next level by adding some sweet and delicious marinated mussels. Don't have the time to marinate your own? No worries, we've done the hard work for you and found the best tinned options out there. Scout, Patagonia, and Matiz Gallego are our top picks. Trust us, this is going to be the talk of the table at your next dinner party.

To make the marinated mussels, in a bowl, combine the mussels, oil, pepper juice, parsley, green onion, garlic, chile, and a pinch each of salt and pepper and mix well. Cover and refrigerate for at least 30 minutes or up to 1 day.

To prepare the toast, preheat the oven to 375ºF.

In a bowl, stir together the tomatoes and oil and season lightly with salt and pepper.

Cut the ciabatta loaf crosswise into 4 equal pieces. Each piece should be about 4 inches wide. Split each piece horizontally to create two 4-inch squares each about 1 inch thick. Arrange the bread, crust side down, on a sheet pan. Drizzle each piece with oil and lightly season with salt and pepper. Bake until lightly golden brown and crispy yet still soft and chewy in the center, 5–7 minutes.

To serve, slather a generous spoonful of the tomato mixture onto each toast, covering the top from edge to edge. Then spoon on the mussels, divvying them up evenly among the pieces. Place the toasts on a serving platter and enjoy.

Makes 8 pieces

FOR THE MARINATED MUSSELS

8 oz cooked mussel meat (fresh cooked or thawed frozen)

2 tablespoons extra-virgin olive oil

1 tablespoon juice from pickled peppers (preferably banana or peperoncino)

2 tablespoons finely chopped fresh flat-leaf parsley

1 green onion, white and green parts, thinly sliced

1 clove garlic, finely grated with a zester

1 tablespoon crushed or finely chopped Calabrian chile

Kosher salt and freshly ground black pepper

FOR THE TOAST

1 lb ripe heirloom tomatoes, finely chopped and drained

3–4 tablespoons extra-virgin olive oil, plus more for drizzling

Kosher salt and freshly ground black pepper

1 loaf crusty ciabatta, about 16 inches long

LOBSTER RÉMOULADE–STUFFED PIQUILLO PEPPERS

The perfect pairing of Spanish flavors and Cajun techniques inspired this dish featuring Atlantic lobster. Roasted and stuffed piquillo peppers (Spanish) and lobster rémoulade (Cajun) come together in a delightful culinary marriage made with easy-to-source roasted piquillo peppers and tinned lobster (we like Scout brand). If you're not in the mood for stuffed peppers, the lobster rémoulade is a great snack to bring on a beach day or picnic. Enjoy it with potato chips or crackers, on lettuce cups, or packed into a toasted brioche roll.

In a bowl, combine the lobster, mayonnaise, ketchup, horseradish, diced celery, chile (if using), hot sauce, celery salt, and ¼ teaspoon black pepper. Set aside a pinch of the green onion for garnish and add the remainder to the bowl. Mix everything together well.

Using a small spoon, such as a demitasse spoon, pack the lobster mixture into the peppers. Arrange the stuffed peppers on a small plate and garnish with the reserved green onion and a few twists of the pepper mill.

Cover and refrigerate until well chilled or up to 1 day before serving.

Makes 8–10 stuffed peppers

6–8 oz cooked lobster meat (fresh cooked, thawed frozen, or tinned), diced

3 tablespoons mayonnaise

1 tablespoon ketchup

1 tablespoon peeled and finely grated fresh horseradish root, or 1 teaspoon prepared horseradish

1 celery rib, diced

1 jalapeño chile, diced (optional)

½ teaspoon Sea Salt–Fermented Red Hot Sauce (page 247) or Crystal extra-hot hot sauce

¼ teaspoon celery salt

Freshly ground black pepper

1 green onion, white and green parts, thinly sliced

1 jar (14 oz) roasted piquillo peppers, drained

SMOKED MACKEREL DIP

While casting some lines along the coasts of Wadmalaw and Seabrook Islands, our neighbor and avid fisherman "Perch" recently informed us that despite his love for catching mackerel, he's hard put to find a recipe that does justice to this rich, fatty fish. Luckily for him, we have the answer. When it comes to cooking oily fish like mackerel, the trick is easy: smoke it hard and whip it into a dip. What's even better is that this recipe can be used with other flavorful finfish, such as sea trout, bluefish, and salmon.

In a food processor, combine the mackerel, lemon zest and juice, green onions, parsley, chile (if using), mustard, celery salt, and pepper and pulse until all the ingredients are finely chopped and well mixed. Transfer the mixture to a bowl and fold in the mayonnaise until fully incorporated. Cover and refrigerate until well chilled or up to 7 days before serving.

For an extra-fancy presentation, we like to serve this dip with fish roe. Spoon the dip into a small serving bowl and make an indentation in the center with the back of a teaspoon. Spoon the roe into the indentation. Serve the dip well chilled with potato chips for scooping. We especially like this dip with Krinkle Cut chips flavored with truffle and sea salt, dill pickle, or salt and fresh ground pepper.

Note: There are a few options for getting your hands on smoked mackerel. You can smoke your own, in which case, check out our recipe for smoking fish on page 213. For store-bought, you can find fresh and tinned. For fresh, Maine-based Ducktrap ships delicious peppered smoked mackerel fillets. For tinned, which is easier to source, Patagonia Provisions packs an extremely delicious smoked mackerel that can be found almost anywhere. Just be sure to drain off the olive oil before proceeding.

Makes 2–6 servings

8 oz smoked mackerel (see Note)

Grated zest and juice of ½ lemon

4 green onions, white and green parts, roughly chopped

1 cup roughly chopped fresh flat-leaf parsley

1 jalapeño chile, roughly chopped (optional)

1 tablespoon Creole Mustard (page 245) or store-bought whole-grain mustard

½ teaspoon celery salt

¼ teaspoon freshly ground black pepper

½ cup mayonnaise

1–2 oz fish roe, such as salmon or trout (optional)

Kettle brand Krinkle Cut or other potato chips, for serving

TINNED FISH

Over half the recipes in this chapter can be prepared with tinned fish, or what is commonly referred to as conserva in Spain and Portugal. There's no doubt that tinned fish is now trending throughout the United States, but it's been a staple on the Iberian Peninsula for generations. In the United States, the heyday of tinned fish seems long gone, with the last operations of the famous Cannery Row of California's Monterey Bay shuttering in 1973. However, in recent years, there has been a resurgence of eating fish from a can in the States. There's a lot to love about tinned fish, and aside from it being exceptionally delicious, our favorite attributes are its convenience, variety, and sustainability.

Some of the hardest-to-find species listed throughout this chapter are available tinned, making them, in reality, not so hard to find. This includes our calls for smoked mussels, conch, chopped clams, mussel meats, smoked mackerel, smoked trout, Atlantic lobster, and even crab.

Seafood is highly perishable and often requires energy-consuming refrigeration to store, and unfortunately, it too often spoils before it can be consumed. Researchers from the Johns Hopkins Center for a Livable Future estimate that nearly 50 percent of the edible US seafood supply, or 2.3 billion pounds, is wasted each year. Some is lost due to bycatch, some is lost in distribution and retail, and a staggering 1.3 billion pounds are lost at the consumer level.

Wasting the edible meat of animals that were removed from their natural ecosystems by humans for human consumption is the antithesis of sustainability—and that's before we consider the waste of other natural resources that went into harvesting these animals with no greater purpose or contribution to the well-being of society (such as the fossil fuels burned to get that fish to your refrigerator). By nature, tinned seafood is preserved and shelf-stable. It won't spoil until opened, and because a pack size is often right around one portion, there is almost never any waste due to leftovers.

SUNBURST SMOKED TROUT DEVILED EGGS

Perhaps we're cut from a different cloth, but we believe that deviled eggs should be a standard at any social gathering. They're quick to make and infinitely delectable. Sourcing quality ingredients is always step number one, so after securing pasture-raised organic chicken eggs, we look to our friends over at Sunburst Trout Farms, who farm trout sustainably in the pristine waters of Shining Rock Wilderness, North Carolina.

To hard-boil eggs, we like to put the eggs in a large pot with water to cover generously, bring the water to a boil over medium-high heat, and set a timer for 12 minutes. When the timer goes off, we immediately shock them in an ice bath for 12 minutes and then peel them under cold running water.

Cut each peeled egg in half lengthwise and separate the yolk from the white. Set the whites aside. Put all the yolks into a food processor along with the trout fillet, mayonnaise, mustard, horseradish, parsley, and pepper and pulse until well mixed. You can keep the mixture somewhat chunky or process it for a smooth filling, whichever you prefer. For a chunkier filling, the stuffing can be mixed in a medium bowl by hand with a fork.

Arrange the egg whites hollow side up on a serving platter and spoon a generous amount of the trout filling into each one. You may have a little left over, which is delicious smeared on a cracker. Spoon a small amount of trout roe on top of each filled egg white and garnish each with a pinch of the chives.

Cover the platter and refrigerate the stuffed eggs just until well chilled before serving. The filling can be made up to 3 days in advance, but we suggest refrigerating the filling and egg whites separately and then stuffing the eggs just before serving.

SUNBURST TROUT FARMS

We've been sourcing from this fine small farm for close to a decade and can attest to the superior quality and flavor of its trout and trout caviar. Founded by Dick Jennings in 1948, this third-generation family farm is currently operated by brothers Wes and Ben Eason, who mindfully consider all aspects of their footprint, from composting to packaging with recyclable materials. They've also mastered the craft of smoking with hickory, so get ready for an authentic treat from the foothills of the Great Smoky and Blue Ridge Mountains. Sunburst Trout Farms' entire lineup of offerings can be purchased through the company website.

Makes 24 deviled eggs

12 pasture-raised organic large eggs

8 oz smoked trout fillet

1 cup mayonnaise

2 tablespoons Creole Mustard (page 245) or store-bought whole-grain mustard

1 tablespoon peeled and finely grated fresh horseradish root, or 1 teaspoon prepared horseradish

1 cup roughly chopped fresh flat-leaf parsley

½ teaspoon freshly ground black pepper

1 oz smoked rainbow trout roe

2 tablespoons thinly sliced fresh chives

Note: There are several options for getting your hands on smoked trout. You can smoke your own, in which case, check out our recipe for smoking fish on page 213. For store-bought, you can find fresh and tinned, with fresh being available in most groceries.

BOTTARGA

Bottarga is a beloved Mediterranean delicacy made by salting, pressing, and then aging the roe sack of the mullet, which is cured in its own natural casing. The result is rich with umami and a brisk essence of the ocean.

This prized preparation is often credited to the Phoenicians of the ancient Levant, who are thought to have introduced it first to Egypt, from which it traveled elsewhere. As they have with many other cured proteins, the Italians have become masters of making bottarga, with recipes dating back to the fifteenth century. We've had the pleasure of learning firsthand about this process while spending time with shepherds on the Mediterranean island of Sardinia. The Sardinians are revered as artisans in the aging and fermenting of a variety of Italian specialties, from bottarga to pecorino to wine. The salty, breezy air combined with the cool reprieve of mountain altitude provide excellent conditions for their craft.

What's fascinating is that a noteworthy amount of bottarga produced in Italy is made from wild mullet caught off the coast of Florida, as these fish are highly prized for the fine quality of their roe. Rightfully so, this is yet another one of our inspirations for infusing coastal Southern cuisine with the flavors, staples, and techniques of Southern Europe.

We love freshly grating bottarga onto any dish that can benefit from a salty pop of umami, such as pizza, pasta, risotto, and even jambalaya. It works wonders on seafood dishes that would typically call for hard-aged cheese, especially where tomatoes are involved.

Bottarga is sold in most Italian markets and can be found near other cured meats that are stored at room temperature. It is shelf-stable until opening and then keeps under refrigeration for up to six months.

SPICY SWORDFISH & CHORIZO MEATBALLS

These succulent spheres are a tasty twist on classic Spanish *albóndigas*—small tapas-style meatballs cooked in a zesty tomato sauce. The mild and meaty swordfish adds a delicious dimension to the dish, while the chorizo provides fat and structure. Make sure that the proteins—swordfish, chorizo, eggs—are cold before they go into the food processor and that you work quickly, as you're creating an emulsion between the protein and fat. The bread helps stabilize and bind. Make these smaller and serve skewered with a toothpick for a traditional *pincho* experience, or make them slightly larger for a meatier indulgence.

In a food processor, combine the swordfish, chorizo, eggs, bread, red pepper flakes, 1 teaspoon salt, and 1/2 teaspoon black pepper and process until they are fully incorporated and the mixture is somewhat smooth, 2–3 minutes.

Have ready a sheet pan. Using your hands, form the mixture into 2-inch balls, and place on the sheet pan. Keep your hands clean by dipping them into cold water after shaping every few meatballs. This will help prevent the mixture from sticking to your hands and make the shaping process much easier.

In a large, deep skillet or sauté pan over medium heat, warm the oil. Working in batches if necessary to avoid crowding, add the meatballs and sear on two or three sides. You're looking for a light golden brown sear here. As the meatballs are ready, transfer them to a plate.

When all the meatballs are seared, add the onion, garlic, and chile to the pan and sweat over medium heat, stirring often, until translucent, 3–5 minutes. Pour in the wine and deglaze the pan, scraping up any browned bits from the pan bottom, then cook until the wine is reduced by half. Add the tomatoes, stir well, bring to a gentle simmer, and season with salt and pepper.

Place the meatballs in the sauce, then cover the pan and simmer gently, adjusting the heat as needed, until the meatballs are cooked through and tender, 30–45 minutes.

Spoon the meatballs and their sauce into a large serving bowl. Garnish with the parsley and freshly grated bottarga (if using) and serve.

Makes 16 meatballs

1 lb swordfish fillet, diced and kept cold

1 lb fresh pork chorizo, casing removed and kept cold

2 large eggs, cold

4 slices white bread, diced

1 teaspoon red pepper flakes

Kosher salt and freshly ground black pepper

1/4 cup extra-virgin olive oil

1/2 yellow onion, diced

4 cloves garlic, thinly sliced

1 Fresno or other medium-hot chile, diced

1/2 cup dry red wine

1 can (28 oz) crushed tomatoes

1/2 cup finely chopped fresh flat-leaf parsley

Bottarga, for grating (optional)

Note: We like to use a fine-rasp Microplane grater to grate the bottarga directly over the meatballs tableside.

HANDHELD

WELCOME TO HANDHELD, WHERE THE ART OF elevated street food is brought to life with regional flavors, chef-driven techniques, and creative Southern renditions. This chapter offers home cooks insight on how we prepare America's most cherished fare, sharing the methods and recipes that helped win us a Michelin Bib Gourmand award. From piled-high sandwiches to po'boys to an epic submarine, each recipe stays true to its roots—be it roadside shack or sidewalk taqueria. Get ready for a mouthwatering experience that promises to satisfy your soul and leave you delightfully messy.

SWORDFISH CUBANO

We first discovered the fish variant of this crispy, crunchy, gooey goody while on an epic Cuban sandwich crawl throughout Miami's Little Havana. While the classic hog-heavy version gets all the glory, this succulent swordfish riff, which marinates the fish in a bright orange mojo, is just as satisfying and vibrant. Crafting your own Creole-style mustard and crunchy dill pickles from scratch is a game changer. And, of course, don't hesitate to use what some would consider way too much cheese.

Lightly season both sides of the swordfish steaks with salt and pepper, then pack them into an airtight container with enough of the mojo to submerge them fully. Refrigerate for at least 1 hour or up to overnight.

Preheat a griddle or large cast-iron skillet over medium-high heat and coat lightly with oil. Add the fish steaks and sear on the first side for about 3 minutes. Flip the steaks, top with the cheese (each sandwich gets 3 cheese slices, so cut and divide evenly among the fish steaks as needed), and cook until nicely seared on the second side and opaque in the center, about 3 minutes longer. When you flip the fish steaks, add the ham to the griddle. The ham will heat up fast and will need to be flipped as well, so keep an eye on it. Remove the fish and ham from the griddle the moment they are ready.

Meanwhile, on the same griddle or pan if there's room or in a separate cast-iron pan if not, toast the exterior sides of the rolls in a little butter. This is essential for getting a classic Cuban sandwich texture, especially since, unlike a traditional Cuban sandwich, this one won't be pressed, as it would overcook the swordfish.

To build the sandwiches, smear 2 tablespoons of the mustard on the bottom half of each roll. Place 2 pieces of swordfish across each mustard-topped half, then stack the ham on top, dividing it evenly. Pile half of the pickles on top of each stack of ham, then close with the roll tops.

Cut the sandwiches in half on the diagonal and serve right away. We typically add more mustard while eating, so keep some close by.

Makes 2 sandwiches

1 swordfish steak, 8–12 oz, cut into 4 equal steaks

Kosher salt and freshly ground black pepper

About 1/2 cup Blood Orange Mojo

Avocado or canola oil, for searing

6 slices Swiss cheese (preferably Cabot or Tillamook)

8 oz smoked deli ham, thinly sliced

2 soft and chewy hoagie rolls, each 8–10 inches long, split horizontally

Salted butter, for toasting the rolls

4 tablespoons Creole Mustard (page 245) or store-bought whole-grain mustard, plus more for serving

1/2 cup dill pickle chips, homemade (page 238) or store-bought

Blood Orange Mojo
Makes 2 cups

1 cup fresh blood orange juice (see Note)
Grated zest and juice of 1 lime
4 cloves garlic
1 green onion, white and green parts, roughly chopped
¼ cup roughly chopped fresh cilantro
1 tablespoon fresh oregano or thyme leaves
1 teaspoon Creole Mustard (page 245) or store-bought whole-grain mustard
½ teaspoon kosher salt
½ cup avocado or canola oil

Note: If you cannot find blood oranges in the market, navel or Valencia can be substituted.

In a blender, combine the orange juice, lime zest and juice, garlic, green onion, cilantro, oregano, mustard, and salt and blend on high speed until smooth, about 1 minute. With the motor running, slowly stream in the oil to emulsify.

Use right away, or transfer to an airtight container and store in the refrigerator for up to 2 weeks. This mojo can be used as a marinade or dressing, adding a zesty punch of citrus and garlic that pairs best with seafood, pork, and chicken.

CARIBBEAN SPINY LOBSTER MULITAS

Drawing on Mexican techniques and Caribbean vibes, these mulitas are one of our favorite street-food riffs of all time. Often described as Mexican grilled cheese, the mulita is made with two corn tortillas, and good-quality maíz (corn) makes *all* the difference. Masa made from whole-kernel heirloom maíz produces rich, hearty tortillas. Here, they soak up heaps of flavor from the lobster and butter. And as the cheese renders into the pan, it merges with the tortilla, creating an outrageously delicious exterior crust. Drag that bad boy through a dollop of our Pineapple Guac and get ready for a bite that's damn near close to everything you've ever wanted.

Lightly season the lobster with salt and pepper. In a large skillet over medium heat, melt 2 tablespoons of the butter. Add the lobster and sauté until fully cooked through, 3–5 minutes. Fold in the green onions, transfer to a small bowl, and set aside.

Wipe the pan clean with a paper towel, place back over medium heat, and melt 2 tablespoons of the butter. Set a sheet pan near the stove. Working in batches appropriate to the size of your skillet, place the tortillas in the pan, top each tortilla evenly with 1 oz (about ¼ cup) of the cheese, and fry until the cheese is melty and the tortilla is light golden brown on the underside, about 2 minutes. Transfer to the sheet pan and repeat, adding more butter to the pan as needed, until all the tortillas are prepared in this fashion.

Distribute the lobster evenly across 4 cheese-topped tortillas and then place a second tortilla, cheese side down, on top. You will have 4 small quesadillas. The next step is what makes a mulita uniquely delicious. Return the skillet to medium heat and melt 2 tablespoons butter. Working in batches, fry each mulita again on both sides until deep golden brown and crispy, about 2 minutes per side, adding more butter to the pan as needed. Be patient and let the color develop. Return the mulitas to the sheet pan as they are ready.

When all the mulitas are ready, cut them in half and serve right away. Accompany them with the guac for dipping and with hot sauce if you like. There's usually plenty of guac, so we often make sure we have tortilla chips to serve alongside as well.

Makes 8 pieces

2 raw Caribbean or Atlantic spiny lobster tails, thawed if frozen, shelled, and meat roughly chopped

Kosher salt and freshly ground black pepper

6 tablespoons salted butter, plus more as needed

2 green onions, white and green parts, thinly sliced

8 heirloom corn tortillas, each 8 inches in diameter

8 oz sharp Cheddar cheese (preferably Cabot or Tillamook), grated (about 2 cups)

Pineapple Guac, for serving

Hot sauce, for serving (optional)

Pineapple Guac
Makes about 2 cups

1 large ripe avocado, halved, pitted, and peeled

½ cup diced fresh or canned pineapple

½ red bell pepper, diced

¼ cup roughly chopped fresh cilantro

1 green onion, white and green parts, thinly sliced

1 serrano chile, finely chopped (optional)

Grated zest and juice of 1 lime

Kosher salt and freshly ground black pepper

In a bowl, combine the avocado, pineapple, bell pepper, cilantro, green onion, chile (if using), and lime zest and juice and mash together with a fork until all the ingredients are well incorporated but the mixture is still somewhat chunky. Season with salt and black pepper, cover, and refrigerate until ready to enjoy.

The guac can be made 1 day in advance and refrigerated in an airtight container that allows for no space between the guac and the lid so oxidation is minimal. You can also press a piece of waxed or parchment paper directly on top of the guac before topping the container with its lid.

THE MIAMI

The cuisine of Miami, which is influenced by a diverse mix of Caribbean cultures, stands out against the "traditional South." This take on a humble grouper sandwich aims to showcase some of those same vibrant flavors of Magic City between two bun halves. The bold jerk seasoning, refreshing mint, punchy lemongrass rémoulade, shaved jalapeño, and splash of fresh lime will bring a South Beach vibe to your table. If you are unable to source grouper, mahi-mahi makes an excellent substitute.

Preheat a cast-iron skillet over medium heat until evenly heated throughout, about 5 minutes. Meanwhile, season each fish fillet on both sides with 1 tablespoon of the jerk seasoning. Then lightly season both sides of each fillet with salt.

When the pan is hot, warm the oil, then gently place the fish in the pan. Sear until golden brown on the first side, 2–3 minutes, then flip the fish and repeat, being mindful not to overcook it. The fish should be golden brown on the second side and just opaque in the center. Transfer the fish to a plate and let rest for 3 minutes.

While the fish rests, place a fresh skillet over medium heat and melt the butter. Add the bun halves cut side down and toast until light golden brown, 1–2 minutes. Transfer the bun halves, cut side up, to individual plates.

In a small bowl, combine the lettuce, mint, jalapeño, and lime zest and juice. Lightly season with salt and mix gently until evenly dressed.

To build the sandwiches, smear 1 tablespoon of the rémoulade on each bun bottom and top. Place the fish on the bun bottoms and dress the bun tops with the lettuce mixture. Divide the tomato slices evenly between the buns, placing them on top of the fish. Close the sandwiches and enjoy.

Makes 2 sandwiches

2 grouper fillets, 6–8 oz each

1 tablespoon Jamaican Jerk Seasoning (page 240)

Kosher salt

2 tablespoons avocado or canola oil

2 tablespoons salted butter

2 gourmet hamburger buns, split

½ cup finely shredded iceberg lettuce

10–12 fresh mint leaves

1 jalapeño chile, thinly sliced

Grated zest and juice of ½ lime

4 tablespoons Ginger Lemongrass Rémoulade (page 244)

1 ripe tomato, sliced

FISH 'N' CHIPS SUBMARINE

We can almost smell the sweet sea air and feel the warm sand between our toes when we bite into this fried fish titan. It's the perfect combination of everything savory and satisfying that you crave after a day at the beach. While we wish it were a menu staple at every seaside joint in the South, we settle for making it ourselves as soon as we return home. Piled high with fish fresh out of the fryer, slaw, crab fries, and more, this sandwich is best enjoyed with a refreshing Savannah Slush (page 39) in hand. Just be warned: this sub is a meal in itself, and eating it might just put you under.

If you're able to get snapper fillets with the tail fin intact, the fin will fry up nice and crispy, making your sandwich even more epic. When preparing this sandwich, we typically source a whole snapper in the 2½- to 3-lb range and fillet it ourselves. This allows us to enjoy the crispy fins, save some money per pound, and stash delicious fish bones in our freezer for future batches of White Wine Fish Stock (page 135).

Marinate the fish as directed in Calabash Style fried seafood.

Before breading and frying the fish, be sure to have all the ingredients prepped and ready for assembly. Pour oil to a depth of 4 inches into a deep fryer or deep, heavy pot and preheat to 350°F. Top a sheet pan with a wire rack and set the pan near the stove.

When the oil is ready, remove the fish fillets from the marinade one at a time; dredge as directed in the Calabash Style instructions, shaking off the excess flour, and carefully lower them into the hot oil. Fry, flipping them halfway through cooking, until golden brown and cooked through, about 7 minutes. Using tongs, transfer them to the wire rack and season immediately with salt and pepper. Drop the fries into the oil and cook for about 3 minutes while the fish rests.

Place the roll halves, cut side up, on individual plates. Smear 2 tablespoons of the mayonnaise on the top half of each roll, then dress the top half with the lettuce, tomatoes, onion, and pickles. If using slaw, spread it across the bottom halves. Pile the fried fish and fries onto the bottom halves, batten down the hatches, and prepare for stealth mode.

Makes 2 sandwiches

2 skin-on snapper fillets, preferably with tail fin intact, 8–12 oz each

Calabash Style fried seafood (page 145)

Neutral oil, for deep-frying

Kosher salt and freshly ground black pepper

2 cups crinkle cut fries

2 soft and chewy hoagie rolls, each 8–10 inches long, split horizontally

4 tablespoons Duke's mayonnaise

1 cup finely shredded iceberg lettuce

2 ripe tomatoes, sliced

½ cup thinly sliced red onion

½ cup dill pickle chips, homemade (page 238) or store-bought

2 cups slaw of choice (optional)

FISH SHACK DOUBLE STACK DELUXE

With its classic Americana vibes, this sandwich is the epitome of the roadside feast. Two cobia burger patties griddled to perfection, draped in melted Cheddar, and stacked on a soft bun with *just* the right number of toppings come together to create something spectacularly nostalgic. This is the kind of food that brings you back to when the stressors of being a grown-up didn't exist. Make sure you have plenty of napkins nearby, and let this gem of a double stack transport you to a carefree time and place.

Preheat a cast-iron skillet over medium heat until evenly heated throughout, about 3 minutes. Meanwhile, lightly season both sides of each patty with salt and pepper.

When the pan is hot, warm the oil, then gently place the patties in the pan. Sear until golden brown on the first side, 2–3 minutes, then flip the patties and top each patty with a slice of cheese. Cook until golden brown on the second side and the cheese is melty, 2–3 minutes. Transfer the patties to a plate and allow to rest for 3 minutes.

While the patties rest, place a fresh skillet over medium heat and melt the butter. Add the bun halves cut side down and toast until light golden brown, 1–2 minutes. Transfer the bun halves, cut side up, to individual plates.

To build the sandwiches, smear 1 tablespoon of the rémoulade on each bun bottom and top. Stack 2 cobia patties on each bun bottom and dress the bun tops with the lettuce and pickles. Close the sandwiches and get ready for a delicious dose of coastal roadside nostalgia.

Makes 2 double stacks

4 Open Blue cobia burger patties, or other sustainable fish burger patties such as salmon or pollock, thawed and patted dry

Kosher salt and freshly ground black pepper

2 tablespoons avocado or canola oil

4 slices mild Cheddar cheese (preferably Cabot or Tillamook)

2 tablespoons salted butter

2 gourmet hamburger buns, split horizontally

4 tablespoons Dill Pickle Rémoulade (page 243)

½ cup finely shredded iceberg lettuce

½ cup dill pickle chips, homemade (page 238) or store-bought

LOUISIANA CRAWFISH ROLL

While the New England lobster roll has earned its place in the global canon of seafood sandwiches, we Southerners know how to put our own spin on things. Enter the Louisiana crawfish roll, a Cajun-inspired rendition bursting with heaps of Deep South glory. An ideal centerpiece for a weekend picnic or brunch, it pairs well with our signature Bloody Mary, the Captain Creole (page 35). Together, they fit like a pair of Ruby Slipper's—there's no place like the Marigny. Right?

In a bowl, combine the crawfish meat, mayonnaise, parsley, celery, green onions, mustard, Cajun seasoning, and zest and juice of ½ lemon and fold together until well mixed. Pack into a food storage container and refrigerate until well-chilled, 2–4 hours or up to 3 days.

When ready to serve, in a skillet over medium heat, melt the butter. Add the buns and toast, turning once, until the tops and bottoms are light golden brown and the buns are steamy when opened. Transfer to individual plates.

In a small bowl, combine the lettuce and remaining 1 tablespoon lemon juice and mix gently.

To build the rolls, pile the lettuce onto the base of each bun, then load up the crawfish salad. Season the tops with a touch more Cajun seasoning and get to the nearest picnic table ASAP.

Makes 2 rolls

1 lb frozen Louisiana crawfish tail meat, thawed, rinsed, and drained

½ cup Duke's mayonnaise

¼ cup finely chopped fresh flat-leaf parsley

1 celery rib, diced

1 green onion, white and green parts, thinly sliced

1 tablespoon Creole Mustard (page 245) or store-bought whole-grain mustard

2 teaspoons Cajun seasoning, homemade (page 240) or store-bought, plus more for serving

Grated zest and juice of ½ lemon, plus 1 tablespoon juice

2 tablespoons salted butter

2 split-top brioche hot dog buns

1 cup finely shredded iceberg lettuce

LOUISIANA CRAWFISH COMPANY

For over thirty-five years, the Louisiana Crawfish Company has been a family-run seafood business based in Natchitoches, Louisiana. Founded by David and Joy McGraw, it started out as a small, family-operated fifty-acre crawfish farm. A major shift took place about fifteen years ago when they passed the torch to their daughter Avery and son-in-law Justin, who've continued to grow the farm to over one thousand acres, all the while increasing their positive impact on the environment and community.

As the demand for live Louisiana-raised crawfish grew and their farming capabilities maxed out, they progressed into being a local distribution hub for countless other small crawfish farmers. But it didn't stop there. Now, the Louisiana Crawfish Company is a one-stop online shop for all things Creole and Cajun, including shellfish, gator, an assortment of regional sausages, seasonings, sweets, party supplies, and even boil equipment.

But to us, what truly sets this company apart is its unwavering commitment to sustainability. Avery and Justin offer local fishers, farmers, and artisans a platform in the global marketplace, supporting their state economy while simultaneously galvanizing a demand for their regional culture and foodways. They also ship with eco-friendly, reusable packaging materials to reduce waste, which should be the golden standard for all food packers and purveyors. Through their best practices in aquaculture and beyond, these folks truly are leading by example in the seafood industry.

Whether you're hosting a crawfish boil or just want to enjoy some of the best seafood and sundries the Gulf Coast has to offer, the Louisiana Crawfish Company is a true treasure.

BLACKENED REDFISH TACOS WITH HOPPIN' JOHN SALSA

Hoppin' John originated in the Gullah Geechee kitchens of the Lowcountry, and despite being widely celebrated throughout the Southeast, it is still somewhat unknown elsewhere. Some traditionalists reserve this dish for New Year's Day, while others consider it the perfect weeknight meal for working-class families. As with any rice-and-beans dish, hoppin' John offers complex carbohydrates and a source of complete protein from the combination of Carolina Gold rice and nutrient-dense cowpeas, crops that were transported from West Africa. For our Hoppin' John Salsa, we use raw, crunchy bell pepper, onion, and celery—aka the holy trinity—as the base and black-eyed peas as the star, which marry deliciously with the bold flavors of the blackened redfish. Frying your tortillas in bacon fat adds a smoky pork layer to your tacos that true hoppin' John demands, but if you don't have any on hand, butter will do just fine.

Prepare the redfish as directed in the blackened fish instructions. While you're blackening the fish, you can simultaneously prepare your tortillas.

Create an aluminum foil pouch to hold the fried tortillas, set it on a sheet pan, and set the pan next to the stove. In a large cast-iron skillet over medium heat, melt the bacon fat. Working in batches to avoid crowding, add the tortillas and fry until golden brown on the first side, about 2 minutes. Flip and repeat. As the tortillas are ready, slip them into the foil pouch to keep warm and continue until all the tortillas are fried.

To build the tacos, slather 1 tablespoon of the rémoulade in a strip across the base of each tortilla. Place a fish strip on each tortilla, spoon on as much salsa as you like, and then top off with the cilantro. Fold the tacos and serve right away.

Makes 8 tacos

1 lb redfish fillets, cut into 8 equal strips (2 oz each)

Perfectly Blackened Fish (page 183)

¼ cup Cajun seasoning, homemade (page 240) or store-bought

4 tablespoons bacon fat or salted butter

8 heirloom corn tortillas, each 6 inches in diameter

½ cup Green Rémoulade (page 243)

Hoppin' John Salsa

1 cup roughly chopped fresh cilantro

Hoppin' John Salsa
Makes about 2 cups

1 cup cooked heirloom black-eyed peas
1 celery rib, diced
½ red bell pepper, diced
½ red onion, diced
1 clove garlic, finely grated with a zester
Grated zest and juice of 1 lemon
¼ cup roughly chopped fresh flat-leaf parsley
Kosher salt and freshly ground black pepper

In a bowl, combine the peas, celery, bell pepper, onion, garlic, parsley, and lemon zest and juice and mix well. Season with salt and black pepper.

The salsa can be served right away but tastes even better the next day. Pack into a food storage container and refrigerate. It will keep for up to 5 days.

FULLY DRESSED OYSTER PO'BOY

The OG po'boy was filled with roast beef bits and gravy, and it was all about high-calorie intake and cheap cost of goods. Today, other iconic fillings have come into play, most of which are of the fried seafood variety. In New Orleans, fully dressed means shredded lettuce, tomatoes, mayonnaise, and pickles. Some of our favorite places in NOLA to grab a po'boy are Killer Poboys, Parkway Bakery & Tavern, and Domilise's Po-boys & Bar.

When making po'boys at home, it is critical to use the right bread. We recommend an 8- to 10-inch-long piece of soft yet chewy French bread, similar in style to a hoagie roll, for each sandwich. You won't find it packaged in the bread aisle. Instead, check near the deli where the freshly baked bread is kept. One more thing, since we're Carolinians and just can't help ourselves, we also add slaw. Don't judge us. It's delicious.

Pour oil to a depth of 4 inches into a deep fryer or deep, heavy pot and heat to 350ºF. Top a sheet pan with a wire rack and set the pan near the stove. Preheat the oven to 375ºF.

While the oil heats, marinate the oysters (see page 146). Note that the oysters don't need to sit in marinade for this particular recipe. Instead, they just need to be fully submerged. Once the oysters are good and wet, move on to the dredging step and pack them firmly into the flour, flipping and repeating.

When the oil is ready, working in batches if needed to avoid crowding, remove the oysters from the flour, shaking off the excess, and carefully lower them into the hot oil. Fry until golden brown and cooked through, about 3 minutes. Using tongs, transfer them to the wire rack, then lightly season with salt and pepper.

We like to slice the roll horizontally about three-fourths of the way through, leaving about 1 inch intact so the sandwich stays together when it is picked up. Po'boys are best when the bread is dry toasted just before they are built, so after slicing, pop the bread into the oven until the outside gets slightly crispy and the inside is warm throughout, 3–5 minutes. This simple technique creates a thin crust around the edges and gets the interior soft and steamy.

To build the po'boys, smear 2 tablespoons of the rémoulade on the top side of each roll, then dress the top side with the lettuce, tomatoes, and pickles. If enjoying with slaw, spread it across the bottom side of each roll. Pile the fried oysters onto the bottom side and *laissez les bons temps rouler!*

Makes 2 po'boys

Neutral oil, for deep-frying

8-oz tub freshly shucked oysters

Kosher salt and freshly ground black pepper

Carolina Cornmeal fried seafood (page 146)

2 soft and chewy hoagie rolls, each 8–10 inches long

4 tablespoons Creole Rémoulade (page 241)

1 cup finely shredded iceberg lettuce

1–2 ripe tomatoes, sliced

1/2 cup dill pickle chips, homemade (page 238) or store-bought

1 cup Pop's Slaw (page 238), optional

Note: Before breading and frying the oysters, be sure to have all the ingredients prepped and ready for assembly.

CALABASH-STYLE ROCK SHRIMP SANDWICH

Sammy here. As a kid, I always looked forward to our family trips to the State Farmers Market in Raleigh, North Carolina. Sure, the produce was rad, but what really got my mouth watering were the fried popcorn shrimp sandwiches at the NC Seafood Restaurant, a Calabash-style fry house on the market grounds. This sandwich is a thing of local legend and deserves to be declared a national treasure. At its heart, it's more like a fried shrimp plate, overflowing with locally sourced seafood and served with a bun, cocktail sauce, tartar sauce, and slaw. Lettuce is probably involved, too, which adds a necessary freshness. Here's my rendition—an ode to the fine folks who've been doing it "the right way" since 1991. Don't forget extra sauce for dipping the shrimp that will inevitably fall out of the bun. It's messy, delicious, and everything you want in a fried shrimp sandwich.

Before breading and frying the shrimp, be sure to have all the ingredients prepped and ready for assembly. Pour oil to a depth of 4 inches into a deep fryer or deep, heavy pot and heat to 350°F. Top a sheet pan with a wire rack and set the pan near the stove.

While the oil heats, marinate the shrimp (page 145). Note that the shrimp don't need to sit in marinade for this particular recipe. Instead, they just need to be fully submerged. Once the shrimp are good and wet, move on to the dredging step and pack them firmly into the flour, flipping and repeating.

When the oil is ready, working in batches if needed to avoid crowding, remove the shrimp from the flour, shaking off the excess, and carefully lower them into the hot oil. Fry, flipping them halfway through cooking, until golden brown and cooked through, about 3 minutes. Using tongs, transfer them to the wire rack. Generously sprinkle them with the Lowcountry seasoning immediately.

In a large skillet over medium heat, melt the butter. Add the bun halves cut side down and toast until light golden brown, 1–2 minutes. Transfer the bun halves, cut side up, to individual plates.

To build the sandwiches, smear 2 tablespoons of the cocktail sauce on the top half of each bun and pile on the lettuce. Spoon 2 tablespoons of the slaw on the bottom half of each bun, then pile on the fried shrimp. Give the shrimp a good squeeze of lemon juice, close the sandwiches, and eat right away.

Makes 2 sandwiches

Neutral oil, for deep-frying

8 oz peeled wild Gulf rock shrimp

Calabash Style fried seafood (page 145)

Lowcountry Boil Seasoning (page 239) or Old Bay Seasoning, for sprinkling

2 tablespoons salted butter

2 gourmet hamburger buns, split horizontally

4 tablespoons Chunky Creole Cocktail Sauce (page 244) or store-bought cocktail sauce

½ cup finely shredded iceberg lettuce

4 tablespoons Cook Out Slaw (page 238) or store-bought slaw

2 lemon wedges

Note: Enjoy with a Pawleys Island Palmer (page 45).

STOCK MARKET

A LOT OF COMFORTING FOOD STARTS WITH A good stock. In the South, a good stock starts with the holy trinity, some garlic, and a handful of this and that. Unfamiliar with the holy trinity of the Southern kitchen? It's the Cajun and Louisiana Creole equivalent of the French mirepoix of onion, celery, and carrot with one big difference: Southern kitchens swap out the carrot for green bell pepper—and that one ingredient swap changes *everything*.

Layering aromatics is the first step toward building any stock and, consequently, any dish. In this chapter, you'll find recipes for stocks made with the intention of using them in Southern cooking, where they add a deep layer of soul and authenticity to any dish. From there, we encourage you to get creative and elevate your favorite Southern classics, including gumbo, crawfish pie, shrimp and grits, regional seafood boils, and even Brunswick stew. The demand for stock is not just limited to the recipes in this chapter, so as you cook through *Salt & Shore*, plan to come back here for guidance until you've mastered stocks.

PAN-ROASTED SHELLFISH STOCK

This is quite possibly our all-time-favorite stock. We freeze our leftover shrimp, lobster, and crab shells until we've got enough to make a batch, but you can also buy shrimp shells at some seafood counters, so just ask the fishmonger. The method for this stock is derived from the classic French technique for brown veal stock, which happens to be the most luxurious stock in recorded history. Here, we pan roast the shellfish shells over medium-high heat with a touch of oil to deepen their sweet, briny flavor. Adding tomato paste toward the end of sweating the mirepoix is a technique called pinçage. The sugars in the tomato paste caramelize and melt into the mirepoix and shells, creating an intensely rich depth.

In an 8- to 12-quart stockpot over medium-high heat, warm 1–2 tablespoons of the oil. Add the shellfish shells and cook, stirring often, until bright red and aromatic, 3–5 minutes. Transfer the shells to a bowl and set aside.

With the pot over medium heat, add the remaining 1–2 tablespoons oil. Add the yellow onion, green peppers, and celery and sweat, stirring often, until translucent, 3–4 minutes. Add the tomato paste and stir until fully incorporated, then cook, stirring frequently, until caramelized to a rich red, 3–5 minutes. This is your pinçage. Pour in the wine and deglaze the pot, scraping up any browned bits (fond) from the pot bottom.

Return the shells to the pot and add the parsley stems, green onions, garlic, bay leaves, peppercorns, salt, and enough water to fill the pot about 85 percent. Bring everything to a simmer, adjust the heat to maintain a gentle simmer, cover, and cook for at least 6 hours or up to overnight.

Remove the pot from the heat and strain the stock through a fine-mesh sieve into a shallow container. Let cool for several minutes, then refrigerate uncovered until fully chilled.

Transfer the stock to airtight containers and refrigerate for up to 5 days or freeze for up to 3 months.

Makes about 4 quarts

2–3 tablespoons avocado oil or other neutral high-heat oil

2 lb shellfish shells, such as shrimp, lobster, or crab, or a mixture

1 yellow onion, diced

2 green peppers, such as bell, poblano, or Anaheim, or a mixture

¼ head celery, diced

2 tablespoons tomato paste

1 cup dry white wine

Stems from 1 bunch fresh flat-leaf parsley

1 bunch green onions, white part only

1 head garlic, unpeeled and smashed

2 bay leaves

1 tablespoon black peppercorns

1 teaspoon kosher salt

4–6 quarts water

LOWCOUNTRY SHRIMP & GRITS

Shrimp and grits is a revered dish that has been adopted by many Southern states as a staple of their cuisine. However, few know of its true origin in the Gullah Geechee communities of the Lowcountry. Gullah Geechee cuisine is a blend of West African, Native American, and European culinary traditions that developed over generations of enslaved Africans and their descendants who worked on the plantations of the coastal regions of South Carolina and Georgia. By honoring the Gullah Geechee roots of shrimp and grits, this recipe invites us to appreciate the cultural contributions of this community to Southern cuisine. Here, we offer our Sunday brunch riff, which features wild Georgia shrimp, a shellfish velouté, and our cheesy grits. The sauce is the stuff that dreams are made of, so be sure to serve plenty of it, and offer lots of freshly sliced crusty bread at the table.

In a large saucepan, combine the stock, cream, 4 tablespoons of the butter, the Worcestershire sauce, bay leaves, Cajun seasoning, and garlic. Attentively bring the mixture to a simmer over medium heat, then immediately adjust the heat to maintain a gentle simmer and cook, whisking frequently, until reduced by half, 30–45 minutes. Remove from the heat, strain through a fine-mesh sieve into a small bowl, and pour back into the saucepan.

Add the shrimp and the remaining 4 tablespoons butter to the pan and place over medium-high heat. Bring to a simmer and cook, stirring frequently so as not to curdle or break the cream, until the shrimp are fully cooked and the sauce is slightly thickened and creamy, 4–5 minutes.

Remove from the heat, taste the sauce for seasoning, and adjust with salt and pepper to your liking. Add the parsley and green onions and fold in just until well mixed. Divide the grits evenly among individual bowls and spoon the shrimp and plenty of sauce on top. Serve immediately with bread for dipping.

Makes 4 servings

2 cups Pan-Roasted Shellfish Stock (page 124), or 1 tablespoon Better Than Bouillon Lobster Base dissolved in 2 cups water

2 cups heavy cream

½ cup (4 oz) salted butter, cut into 1-tablespoon pats

1 tablespoon Worcestershire sauce

2 bay leaves

2 teaspoons Cajun seasoning, homemade (page 240) or store-bought

1 tablespoon minced garlic

2 lb wild Georgia shrimp (21/25), peeled and deveined

Kosher salt and freshly ground black pepper

¼ cup finely chopped fresh flat-leaf parsley

¼ cup thinly sliced green onions, white and green parts

Cacio e Pepe Grits (page 237)

Crusty bread, for serving

ANCHORED SHRIMP CO.

The story of Anchored Shrimp Co. is a tale of perseverance and dedication to a way of life passed down through three generations of Georgia shrimpers. Aaron Wallace's paternal grandfather, Alfred, was a shipbuilder, and his boats still ply the waters of the Georgia coast. Aaron's father, John, built his first shrimping boat at age twenty, and today that vessel, the *Gale Force* (named after Aaron's mother), is in operation alongside a fleet of independent Georgia shrimpers.

In 2013, the Wallace family purchased Poteet Seafood Company, a business that had supported the Georgia shrimping industry for nearly four decades. Aaron has since rebranded the company as Anchored Shrimp Co., expanded its processing capacity, and opened a seafood market. Anchored Shrimp Co. is now the state's largest certified wild Georgia shrimp seller. Despite this achievement, less than 10 percent of Georgia restaurants selling seafood source wild Georgia shrimp.

As the saying goes, "Shrimpin' ain't easy." Small, independent shrimping operations such as Anchored Shrimp Co. face numerous challenges, including competition from large corporations and cheap overseas imports. These rivals often have significantly greater resources and can outsource labor and import product, making it difficult for small-scale operations to compete. Independent shrimpers must also navigate a complex web of regulations and fees, which can be a barrier to entry for new businesses.

Despite these challenges, Aaron Wallace and his family are committed to preserving the legacy of the Georgia shrimping industry. They embody the very essence of what it takes to own an American small business. When he's not packing shrimp or picking up the phone, Aaron is driving truck routes throughout the state, personally ensuring the safe delivery of his precious cargo. Even as he manages the day-to-day operations of Anchored Shrimp Co., he still gets out on the boats from time to time to shrimp.

The fleet of independent shrimping boats—twelve in total—that supply Anchored Shrimp Co. is docked in picturesque McIntosh County, Georgia. Its seafood market is open to the public and is located in Brunswick, Georgia, a city with a diverse economy that still values its ties to the seafood industry.

By supporting independent shrimpers like the Wallace family and their cohorts, we can help ensure that the legacy of the Georgia shrimping industry continues for generations. Policymakers can also play a role by advocating for guidelines that protect small-scale fishing operations and promote sustainable fishing practices. By working together, we can preserve the unique culture and way of life passed down through generations of Georgia shrimpers and ensure the long-term viability of this vital industry.

SHELLFISH GUMBO POT

Sammy here. I'm about to say something controversial. There's no roux in my gumbo. Many might think that a gumbo without roux is no gumbo at all, but tastiness simply cannot be argued with. The purpose of any roux is to create texture, depth, stability, and consistency; but when preparing this gumbo, I rely on other culinary techniques to achieve those characteristics. The thickening agents of this gumbo are purely vegetal and come from okra, filé powder, and tomato paste. My inspiration lies within my Lebanese heritage, as I feel as though gumbo is a dish that should be made with unique accents of family ancestry. If you'd like to add a roux, omit the tomato paste and cut the okra amount in half.

In an 8-quart Dutch oven over medium heat, melt 4 tablespoons of the butter. Add the onions, celery, chiles, and garlic and sweat, stirring frequently, until translucent, 5–7 minutes. Add the tomato paste and stir until fully incorporated, then cook, stirring frequently, until caramelized to a rich red, 3–5 minutes. This is your pinçage. Pour in the wine and deglaze the pot, scraping up any browned bits (fond) from the pot bottom.

Add the stock, okra, bay leaves, Worcestershire sauce, and Cajun seasoning, stir well, and bring everything to a simmer. Taste and lightly season with salt. Turn down the heat to a gentle simmer, cover, and cook, stirring every 15 minutes or so, until the okra is tender and not mucilaginous (slimy), about 1 hour.

When the okra is tender enough to break up by stirring with a wooden spoon, it's done. Taste for salt again and season to your liking if needed, keeping in mind that the mussels and oysters (if using) will add a substantial layer of oceanic salinity. Your gumbo base is done. You can keep it on very low heat for a bit until you're ready to finish the gumbo, or you can cool and refrigerate it for up to 2 days, then reheat it over low heat before continuing. You'll want to finish the gumbo just before serving to preserve the plumpness of the shellfish.

To finish, dust the filé powder over the base, stirring to avoid clumping. Add the mussels, shrimp, and oysters (if using) and stir until incorporated. Turn up the heat to medium-high and cover the pot. Cook until the mussels open, 7–12 minutes.

Serve immediately family-style, discarding any mussels that failed to open. We often place our Dutch oven on a trivet in the center of our table. Accompany with rice, hot sauce, and crusty bread.

Makes 6–8 servings

½ cup (4 oz) salted butter

1 cup diced yellow onions

1 cup diced celery

1 cup diced Anaheim or poblano chile

2 tablespoons minced garlic

2 tablespoons tomato paste

1 cup dry white wine

8 cups Pan-Roasted Shellfish Stock (page 124), or 5 tablespoons Better Than Bouillon Lobster Base dissolved in 8 cups water

2 lb okra, tops removed

2 fresh or dried bay leaves

1 tablespoon Worcestershire sauce

1 tablespoon Cajun seasoning, homemade (page 240) or store-bought

Kosher salt

2 tablespoons filé powder

3 lb Atlantic mussels, scrubbed and debearded

1 lb head-on wild Atlantic or Gulf shrimp (12/15)

12–24 oysters, shucked and kept on the half shell (page 70), optional

Hot steamed Carolina Gold rice, for serving

Hot sauce, for serving

Crusty bread, for serving

GUMBO

Gumbo, a quintessential Southern dish, encapsulates the region's diverse culinary heritage and showcases the creativity of its cooks throughout history. This rich and flavorful stew has roots debated between West African and Choctaw influences, evidenced by the etymology of the words "gombo" and "kumbo" in their respective cultures, both referring to ingredients used in gumbo-like stews.

Okra, a key gumbo ingredient, has been a thickening agent in African soups for centuries and found its way to the Americas through enslaved West Africans. Filé powder, another common gumbo component, has Native American origins, with the Choctaw using ground sassafras leaves for seasoning and thickening.

Even in the city of New Orleans, ground zero for gumbo, the dish varies greatly within the same family tree. The many variations include seafood, chicken, and sausage, and there's even a vegetarian gumbo. Each gumbo recipe has its own unique flavor profile, spices, and ingredients.

Perhaps attempting to prove its origin or what deems a gumbo's legitimacy isn't quite as important as acknowledging why we cook gumbo, why we eat it, and what the people behind this beloved dish have endured throughout the history of the United States. Gumbo is a dish born of hardship and ingenuity, created by people who used the ingredients they had available to them to put together something delicious and nourishing. It has evolved over the centuries, reflecting the cultural influences of the people who have cooked and enjoyed it.

In many ways, gumbo is a microcosm of the South itself, with its diverse cultural influences and the resilience of the people who call it home. It is a dish that brings people together, evoking memories of family, community, and tradition. Whether you favor a chocolate roux or a vegetarian gumbo, one thing is certain: this beloved Southern stew will continue to bring joy and comfort to generations of cooks for years to come.

CHARLESTON PERLOO

Perloo, also spelled *purloo* and *purlow* (and pronounced puhr-loe), is a one-pot rice-based dish with complex origins and etymology that can be traced back to Persia. Its preparation methods share similarities with many other treasured dishes found in regions where rice farming has historically provided a way of life. However, it was enslaved Africans who introduced it to the South in the form that we know and celebrate today.

Lowcountry perloo, a characteristic dish of the Carolina rice kitchen, bears a striking resemblance to West African jollof. The Carolina rice kitchen emerged in the early nineteenth century amongst enslaved Africans who cultivated and cooked Carolina Gold rice. This legacy is one of sustainability, community, creativity, and a dependence on a complex agricultural system suited to local conditions and cultural needs. It is not a physical place but a unique cuisine that reflects a melting pot of cultures and embodies the history of the region.

The essential element of perloo is delicate, nonaromatic long-grain rice cooked in a rich broth and layered with a variety of aromatics, tomatoes, meats, poultry, and seafood. The rice grains must be cooked to nearly dry, with no residual liquid, and must remain separate. Our recipe offers a unique take on the classic while highlighting the rich cultural history behind the dish. We combine savory seafood and the holy trinity of onion, celery, and pepper with accents from around the Mediterranean to create a perloo that is elegant enough for any special occasion yet comforting enough to be enjoyed family-style at your next Sunday supper.

In a large saucepan over medium heat, combine the stock and crushed tomatoes and bring to a gentle simmer. Taste and lightly season with salt and pepper to your liking.

In a Dutch oven or 14-inch cast-iron skillet over medium heat, melt 2 tablespoons of the butter. Add the yellow onion, celery, chile, and garlic and sweat, stirring frequently, until translucent, 3–5 minutes. Add the tomato paste and stir until fully incorporated, then cook, stirring frequently, until caramelized to a rich red, 3–5 minutes. This is your pinçage.

Recipe continues

Makes 4–6 servings

8 cups Pan-Roasted Shellfish Stock (page 124), or 5 tablespoons Better Than Bouillon Lobster Base dissolved in 8 cups water

2 cups canned crushed tomatoes

Kosher salt and freshly ground black pepper

4 tablespoons salted butter, cut into 1-tablespoon pats

½ cup finely diced yellow onion

½ cup finely diced celery

½ cup finely diced poblano chile

2 tablespoons minced garlic

2 tablespoons tomato paste

2 cups Carolina Gold rice

1 cup dry white wine

2 fresh or dried bay leaves

12 oz andouille sausage, sliced on the diagonal ¼ inch thick

1 lemon, halved

Avocado oil, for the lemon

1 lb wild Georgia shrimp (21/25), peeled and deveined

½ cup roughly chopped fresh flat-leaf parsley

½ cup thinly sliced green onions, white and green parts

12–18 oysters, shucked and kept on the half shell (page 70), optional

STOCK MARKET

Add the rice and sweat, stirring frequently, until the kernels are translucent around the edges, 2–3 minutes. Add the wine, bay leaves, and a fat pinch of salt and cook, stirring frequently, until the wine is fully absorbed, 2–3 minutes.

Reduce the heat to medium-low. Working in roughly 2-cup increments, begin adding the stock mixture and cook, stirring somewhat frequently, until the liquid is absorbed by the rice before adding the next addition. Add the andouille along with the second round of the stock mixture.

Meanwhile, char the lemon. Preheat a small cast-iron skillet over medium heat for 3 minutes. Lightly season the cut side of each lemon half with oil, salt, and pepper. Place the halves, flesh side down, in the hot pan and cook until the edges start to blacken, 3–5 minutes. Remove from the pan and set aside.

When it's time to add the final round of the stock mixture to the rice mixture, add the shrimp, the remaining 2 tablespoons butter, the parsley, and the green onions, reserving a pinch each of the parsley and green onions for garnish. Gently fold all the ingredients together, place a lid on the pot, and reduce the heat to low. Cook until the shrimp are done, 6–8 minutes. If adding oysters, shingle them into the rice mixture about 3 minutes before the shrimp are finished cooking. Expect our perloo preparation to be slightly saucy, as its method is derived from paella, risotto, and jollof.

Garnish with pepper, the reserved parsley and green onion, and the charred lemon. We like to serve this dish family-style, placing the pot on a trivet in the center of the table.

Sourcing Quality Shrimp

For a handful of reasons, sourcing quality shrimp is more challenging than sourcing any other shellfish. Our litmus test is to check for one ingredient that should never be included on the label: sodium tripolyphosphate (STPP). This chemical emulsifier is added to make shrimp retain moisture, making them larger and glossy. It essentially swells them up so you think you're buying bigger, better shrimp when you're actually just paying for water weight. Plus, this harmful compound imparts a bitter, soapy flavor to your shrimp. The added moisture is leached out during the cooking process, which results in both steaming your shrimp and overcooking them. It's also the culprit in many broken pan sauces.

If you've ever wondered, "How did I overcook my shrimp so fast?" as you attempt to enjoy a bowl of shrunken, chewy critters, know that it wasn't your fault. It was the fault of sodium tripolyphosphate. From what we've learned over the years, if you source shrimp that is bona fide sustainable *and* doesn't contain STPP, you're in for a delicious treat.

WHITE WINE FISH STOCK

Here, we have fused the flavors of the Southern kitchen with classic French technique to offer a hearty yet elegant stock base for seafood soups, stews, and chowders. We love buying whole fish that (after filleting) yield rich, meaty bones for stock. Usually, one to two fish will provide enough flavor for a batch, and if we're not quite ready to simmer one up, we'll freeze the heads and bones until we are.

In an 8- to 12-quart stockpot over medium-high heat, combine the fish bones and heads, wine, yellow onions, peppers, celery, garlic, parsley stems, green onions, bay leaves, peppercorns, salt, and enough water to cover all the ingredients by 4 inches. Bring everything to a simmer, adjust the heat to maintain a gentle simmer, cover, and cook for at least 6 hours or up to overnight.

Remove the pot from the heat and strain the stock through a fine-mesh sieve into a shallow container. Let cool for several minutes, then refrigerate uncovered until fully chilled.

Transfer the stock to airtight containers and refrigerate for up to 5 days or freeze for up to 6 months.

Note: To freeze the stock so it takes up less space in the freezer, pour it into a large saucepan, bring to a simmer over medium heat, and cook, uncovered, until reduced to 2 cups, about 45 minutes. Remove from the heat, let cool, then pour into ice-cube trays and freeze. Once the stock cubes are frozen, pop them from the trays and put them into a resealable plastic freezer bag or airtight container and store in the freezer for up to 6 months. Each ice cube will yield roughly 1 cup stock. To use, dilute each thawed cube with enough water to equal 1 cup.

Makes about 4 quarts

3–5 lb fish bones and heads, well rinsed and gills trimmed off

4 cups dry white wine

2 yellow onions, unpeeled and roughly chopped

3 green peppers, such as bell, poblano, or Anaheim, or a mixture, roughly chopped

¼ head celery, roughly chopped

1 head garlic, unpeeled and smashed

Stems from 1 bunch fresh flat-leaf parsley

1 bunch green onions, white part only

2 fresh or dried bay leaves

1 tablespoon black peppercorns

1 teaspoon kosher salt

3–5 quarts water

WAHOO BRUNSWICK STEW

Brunswick is a coastal community of Georgia, which makes Brunswick stew all the better to make with seafood. Wahoo, which is line caught off the Georgia coast—and along the southeastern Atlantic—plays beautifully in this dish. Its texture is somewhat firm and meaty yet also sweet and delicate, with a full flavor that tastes unlike any other white-fleshed fish we've had. If you can't get your hands on wahoo, we recommend mahi-mahi, black sea bass, triggerfish, cobia, monkfish, and even Atlantic salmon.

In a Dutch oven over medium heat, warm the oil. Add the yellow onion, celery, chile, and garlic and sweat, stirring frequently, until translucent, 3–5 minutes. Add the okra, potatoes, tomatoes, stock, bay leaves, Worcestershire sauce, hot sauce, and Cajun seasoning (if using) and bring to a simmer, stirring somewhat frequently. Reduce the heat to maintain a gentle simmer, taste for seasoning, and adjust with salt and pepper to your liking. Cover and cook, stirring occasionally, until the potatoes and okra are tender, 30–45 minutes.

Add the lima beans, corn, parsley, and green onions and stir until well incorporated. To finish, lightly season the fish pieces on both sides with salt and pepper and gently place them in the pot, submerging each piece about two-thirds of the way into the stew. Re-cover the pot and poach the fish until fully cooked, 3–5 minutes.

Serve immediately. We enjoy this stew with a freshly baked skillet of our Lowcountry Cast-Iron Corn Bread (page 233).

Makes 2–4 servings

2 tablespoons avocado oil

1 yellow onion, diced

2 celery ribs, diced

1 poblano chile, diced

2 tablespoons minced garlic

2 cups thick-sliced okra, in ½-inch-thick coins

2 cups diced Yukon Gold potatoes

1 can (28 oz) crushed tomatoes

4 cups fish stock, homemade (page 135) or store-bought

2 fresh or dried bay leaves

1 tablespoon Worcestershire sauce

2 tablespoons Louisiana-style red hot sauce

1 teaspoon Cajun seasoning, homemade (page 240) or store-bought (optional)

Kosher salt and freshly ground black pepper

1 cup fresh, frozen, or canned baby green lima beans

1 cup fresh or frozen corn kernels

1 cup roughly chopped fresh flat-leaf parsley

3 green onions, white and green parts, thinly sliced

1 lb wahoo fillets, cut into 1½-inch pieces

SMOKED OYSTER & BUTTERNUT SQUASH CHOWDER

Chowder is undoubtedly America's favorite seafood soup, and this Southern riff on the New England classic is the stuff that bread bowls were made for. Oftentimes, we crave chowder during cold-weather months, so it only felt right to give y'all a seasonal take. Traditionally, true chowder *must* be prepared with a form of pork product, be it bacon, fatback, or salt pork. Here, we omit the hog and rely on the richness of smoked oysters to create a bold, hearty depth. We call for butternut squash in place of potatoes, and garnish with toasted pumpkin seeds and brown butter sage rather than croutons or oyster crackers. The result is joyous, embodying all the cozy characteristics needed to satisfy your soul throughout the holiday season and beyond.

In a Dutch oven over medium heat, melt 6 tablespoons of the butter. Add the leek, bell pepper, celery, and garlic and sweat, stirring frequently, until translucent, 3–5 minutes. Dust the flour over the vegetable mixture while stirring constantly to avoid lumping, then continue to stir frequently until the flour cooks to a light golden and has a biscuity aroma, 3–5 minutes.

Slowly pour in the stock and wine while stirring constantly to prevent lumps from forming, then deglaze the pot, scraping up any browned bits (fond) from the pot bottom. Add the squash, oysters, and bay leaves, bring to a gentle simmer, and taste for seasoning, adjusting with salt and black pepper to your liking. Reduce the heat to maintain a gentle simmer, cover, and cook, stirring somewhat frequently, until the squash is tender, 30–45 minutes.

Meanwhile, fry the sage leaves for garnish. Line a plate with a few layers of paper towels and set it near the stove. In a large skillet over medium heat, melt the remaining 2 tablespoons butter. Lay the sage leaves in the pan in a single layer and panfry until the butter begins to brown and the sage becomes deep golden brown and aromatic, 2–3 minutes. Quickly remove the pan from the heat and pour the contents onto the towel-lined plate. Lightly season the leaves with salt. As the leaves cool, they will become crispy. We find that brown butter sage adds a charming warmth to our home cooking all autumn and winter long.

Ladle the chowder into individual bowls, garnish with the sage and pumpkin seeds, and serve right away. If the spirit moves you, this is a mighty fine chowder for a bread bowl.

Makes 2–4 servings

½ cup (4 oz) salted butter

1 cup diced leek, white and green parts

1 cup diced green bell pepper

1 cup diced celery

2 tablespoons minced garlic

⅓ cup all-purpose flour

4 cups fish stock, homemade (page 135) or store-bought

1 cup dry white wine

4 cups peeled and diced butternut squash

6–9 oz canned smoked oysters (preferably Ekone), roughly chopped

2 fresh or dried bay leaves

Kosher salt and freshly ground black pepper

12–15 fresh sage leaves

¼ cup toasted pumpkin seeds, for garnish

Note: This method of adding flour to vegetables cooked in fat is a classic French technique called *singer* (sohn-jay), and you're essentially making a roux. It works great for chowders as well as other creamy soups and gravies.

BACKYARD SHELLFISH BOILS

Backyard shellfish boils are hyper-regional throughout the South, varying from town to town and even family to family. Heck, folks even fuss about how to boil, how to season, and, as silly as it sounds, how to eat a backyard shellfish boil. The use of corn and potatoes is standard across the board, and blue crab is always welcome. From there, shellfish species, seasonings, and sausage recommendations vary by location. Inspired by our travels and experiences, we've created recipes for what we consider to be the three most distinct regions where backyard boils are considered a culinary tradition: the Lowcountry, the Gulf Coast of Florida, and Louisiana.

There are, of course, a few things that can be agreed on with any backyard shellfish boil. We recommend you serve your boil family-style and spread it out over a large table covered with newspaper or butcher paper. Enjoy it with plenty of condiments, from drawn butter to a variety of hot sauces, rémoulades, and cocktail sauces. Ice-cold libations are a must and should be kept close at hand during all times. And, of course, don't forget the napkins—rolls of eco-friendly paper towels for guests to tear often do the trick.

ALL-PURPOSE BACKYARD BOIL STOCK

Large pot boils such as this recipe require a powerful heat source. We recommend using a high-output outdoor propane burner or cooking over an open fire. Whichever you choose, always cook with caution and be mindful of your surroundings. In a 20- to 28-quart brazier over high heat, combine the onions, green peppers, celery, garlic, salt, peppercorns, bay leaves, Zatarain's boil mix, and enough water to cover all the ingredients by 4 inches. Bring to a simmer, adjust the heat to maintain a gentle simmer, and cook for 30 minutes.

The first ingredient that goes into the boil is the potatoes. From that point, it's a layering game dependent on the cook time of your other ingredients. When cooking at a gentle simmer, which we recommend, medium-size potatoes take 22–30 minutes to cook. We recommend adding sausage 7–10 minutes before the potatoes are expected to be done, adding corn 5–7 minutes before the potatoes are expected to be done, and adding the shellfish 4–5 minutes before the potatoes are expected to be done. The exception to the shellfish guideline is crab, which we recommend adding at the same time as the sausage.

Serves 4–24

2 yellow onions, unpeeled and roughly chopped

3 green peppers, such as bell, poblano, or Anaheim, or a mixture, roughly chopped

1 head celery, halved crosswise

1 head garlic, unpeeled and smashed

1 tablespoon kosher salt

1 tablespoon black peppercorns

2 fresh or dried bay leaves

1 bag (3 oz) Zatarain's Crawfish, Shrimp & Crab Boil

12–15 quarts water

Lowcountry Shrimp Boil

Makes 4–6 servings

Also known as Frogmore stew, our Lowcountry boil centers on wild Georgia shrimp, andouille sausage, and our very own Lowcountry Boil Seasoning, which, as you'll discover throughout this book, goes great on just about anything.

All-Purpose Backyard Boil Stock (page 139)
12 medium Yukon Gold or Red Bliss potatoes
2–3 lb andouille sausage
1–2 Atlantic blue crabs per person (optional)
6 ears corn, shucked and halved crosswise
5 lb medium or large shell-on wild Georgia shrimp
½ cup Lowcountry Boil Seasoning (page 239)

Make the boil stock as directed, then follow the layering instructions. For this particular boil, we like to toss the shrimp in the boil seasoning 1 hour before the shrimp goes into the pot, as it seeps into the flesh and makes the shrimp extra tasty.

Floribbean Clam Boil

Makes 4–6 servings

Don't sleep on Florida now y'all—they go hard too! This boil is a fabulous way to celebrate the dynamic and diverse flavors of Florida, combining the sweet taste of fresh clams (we like top necks) with wild boar sausage and jerk seasoning.

All-Purpose Backyard Boil Stock (page 139)
½ cup Jamaican Jerk Seasoning (page 240)
12 medium Yukon Gold or Red Bliss potatoes
2–3 lb wild boar sausage
1–2 Atlantic blue crabs per person (optional)
6 ears corn, shucked and halved crosswise
10 lb clams

Make the boil stock as directed. For this particular variation, we like to add the jerk seasoning at the very beginning of preparing the boil when we add the Zatarain's boil. Then follow the layering instructions. Be sure to clean your clams ahead of time. We soak them in ice water dusted with a tablespoon of cornmeal and a pinch of kosher salt in the refrigerator for at least 4 hours to help them purge any sand.

Louisiana Crawfish Boil

Makes 4–6 servings

Louisiana is famous for its festive crawfish boils. From Mardi Gras to Memorial Day, the height of crawfish season in Louisiana is a time of celebration and neighborhood gathering. Heavy doses of Cajun or Creole seasoning are a must, and for us, we enjoy pairing our mudbugs with another Louisiana specialty—smoked boudin sausage.

All-Purpose Backyard Boil Stock (page 139)
2–3 cups Cajun seasoning, homemade (page 240) or store-bought
3–5 lb live Louisiana crawfish (preferably from Louisiana Crawfish Company) per person
12 medium Yukon Gold or Red Bliss potatoes
2–3 lb smoked boudin sausage (pork, alligator, or seafood)
1–2 Atlantic blue crabs per person (optional)
6 ears corn, shucked and halved crosswise

Make the boil stock as directed. For this particular variation, we like to add 1 cup of the Cajun seasoning at the very beginning of preparing the boil when we add the Zatarain's boil.

With the boil stock at a rolling boil, add the crawfish and cook until bright red, 3-5 minutes. Using a spider or other large perforated utensil, scoop them out into a large bowl or other vessel, generously dusting them with the remaining Cajun seasoning (adjusting the amount to the quantity of crawfish) as you do. Pour contents of the bowl into an insulated, hard chest cooler, close and latch tight, and allow the crawfish to "cooler cook" for 15 minutes. Since an insulated, hard chest cooler is designed to maintain its internal temperature, it locks in the heat of the crawfish and boil ingredients, which in turn allows them to gently steam-rest, tenderize, and absorb the flavors of the seasoning. This is also a helpful technique for storage and for keeping things fresh, since serious boilers are known to devour upward of 5 lb of crawfish on their own, which means you'll likely be boiling the crawfish in batches.

FISH CAMP

NOT STRICTLY A COASTAL TRADITION, FISH CAMPS are located throughout the South, where they have been a hallmark of family togetherness for generations. But once a common sight, they are now a dying breed. Never say die! We're here to honor their legacy and preach the gospel of good cooking, and to uphold the beloved Friday-night fish fry culture that's worshipped throughout the Bible Belt. We're taking you on a journey from the Mississippi Delta all the way to the mecca of fried fish in Calabash, North Carolina. Our recipes are technique driven, offering a "choose your own adventure" for preparing the ultimate fried seafood platter with all the fixins. So strap in and get ready for an extra-crispy joyride.

Seafood Frying Chart

When preparing a variety of deep-fried seafood, we find it helpful to have a guide for cooking times based on species, size, and temperature. We've arranged this chart in order of fry time, and for the most part, the guidelines will deliver a foolproof fish fry. We urge you to practice caution when deep-frying. Frying in smaller batches will take longer, but it helps ensure the oil maintains the desired set temperature and prevents the oil from overflowing the pot sides. As always, we recommend cooking attentively, with intuition and intention.

FISH OR SEAFOOD	FRY TEMPERATURE	FRY TIME
Shrimp, Scallops, Oysters, Clams, Squid, Crawfish Tail Meat, whole small pelagic fish (smelt, sardines, etc., and Finfish Nuggets 1½–2 inches in size)	350°F	3–5 minutes
Head-On Shrimp, Soft-Shell Crabs, Finfish Strips, and Fillets weighing 4–12 oz, and Whole Fish weighing 8 oz–1 lb	350°F	5–7 minutes
Whole Fish weighing 1–1½ lb	350°F	7–12 minutes

CALABASH STYLE

Over the past fifty years, the small fishing town of Calabash, North Carolina, has become famous for its light style of frying seasonal seafood harvested along the Carolina coast. For folks like us, making the trek to this regional fried-fish mecca for day-boat delights feels sacred, and certainly satisfies the soul. Myrtle Beach, located just twenty-five miles south of Calabash, has been instrumental in popularizing the renowned Calabash-style seafood with the masses. With its local economy driven by nearly twenty million tourists annually and boasting over a dozen Calabash-style seafood restaurants, visitors to Myrtle Beach and residents alike cannot escape the road signs, billboards, and local radio ads enticing them to indulge in this deep-fried delicacy. Rightfully so, this style of frying has become our "old faithful." It works wonders on all forms of shellfish and finfish, and also happens to be the recipe we most often rely on for frying chicken.

To make the marinade, in a large bowl, whisk together the buttermilk, eggs, and salt until smooth. Add the seafood, stir gently to coat evenly, and pack into an airtight food storage container. Refrigerate for at least 1 hour or up to overnight.

To cook, following the directions included with the Seafood Frying Chart on opposite page, ready the oil for deep-frying.

To prepare the dredge, set a large sheet pan, preferably topped with a wire rack, on your work surface. Using your hands or a sifter to ensure there are no clumps, add the flour to a large bowl. Working with a few pieces at a time, remove the seafood from the marinade and drop into the flour. Bury the seafood in the flour and press down firmly to pack on the coating. Then carefully remove the seafood pieces from the flour, lightly shaking them to remove any excess flour, and place in a single layer on the rack or directly on the pan. Continue until all the seafood is dredged, making sure not to stack the coated pieces, as they may stick together.

Fry the seafood in batches as directed in the Seafood Frying Chart (opposite page). Immediately upon removing the pieces from the oil, season them with your choice of seasoning and serve.

Makes breading for 3–5 lb seafood

FOR THE MARINADE

2 cups buttermilk

5 large eggs

1 teaspoon kosher salt

FOR THE DREDGE

4 cups self-rising flour

3–5 lb seafood of choice

Neutral oil, for deep-frying

Seasoning of choice

CAROLINA CORNMEAL

If you're looking for that classic Southern-style fish fry, our Carolina Cornmeal preparation is exactly that. The marinade of buttermilk and whole eggs tenderizes while adding tang, and the simple fifty-fifty blend of our dredge provides a sturdy cornmeal crunch with just enough self-rising flour to fill in all the nooks and crannies. If you'd like to make this preparation gluten-free, skip the flour and use all cornmeal.

To make the marinade, in a large bowl, whisk together the buttermilk, eggs, and salt until smooth. Add the seafood, stir gently to coat evenly, and pack into an airtight food storage container. Refrigerate for at least 1 hour or up to overnight.

To cook, following the directions included with the Seafood Frying Chart on page 144, ready the oil for deep-frying.

To prepare the dredge, set a large sheet pan, preferably topped with a wire rack, on your work surface. Using your hands or a sifter to ensure there are no clumps, add the cornmeal and flour to a large bowl, mixing them well. Working with a few pieces at a time, remove the seafood from the marinade and drop into the dredge. Bury the seafood in the dredge and press down firmly to pack on the coating. Then carefully remove the pieces from the dredge, lightly shaking them to remove any excess dredge, and place in a single layer on the rack or directly on the pan. Continue until all the seafood is dredged, making sure not to stack the coated pieces, as they may stick together.

Fry the seafood in batches as directed in the Seafood Frying Chart. Immediately upon removing the pieces from the oil, season them with your choice of seasoning and serve.

Makes breading for 3–5 lb seafood

FOR THE MARINADE

2 cups buttermilk

5 large eggs

1 teaspoon kosher salt

FOR THE DREDGE

2 cups fine-grind heirloom yellow cornmeal

2 cups self-rising flour

3–5 lb seafood of choice

Neutral oil, for deep-frying

Seasoning of choice

CAROLINA CORN REVIVAL

Call us biased, but as Carolinians, we believe that North and South Carolina are home to the finest grain mills in the United States, and in these parts, corn is king. The Carolinas are known for their colorful array of heirloom corn varieties, including white, yellow, blue, Guinea Flint, Pencil Cob, Henry Moore, and Jimmy Red. These flavorful and nutritious grains are a true taste of the Carolinas, and we're proud to be corn-fed.

The revival of heirloom corn planting and milling throughout the Carolinas today would not have happened without Glenn Roberts of Columbia, South Carolina–based Anson Mills, a key player in preserving and promoting a multitude of heirloom grains long found in the region. Roberts began researching and growing nearly extinct varieties of Southern mill corn in the late 1990s. He also rediscovered the technique of cold milling, which helps preserve the nutrients and flavor of the grains. While the significant contributions of Roberts and Anson Mills cannot be overstated, there are plenty of other Carolina mills worth trying. Some of our favorites include Marsh Hen Mill (Edisto Island, SC), Colonial Milling Co. (Pauline, SC), Farm & Sparrow (Mars Hill, NC), and Atkinson Milling Company (Selma, NC).

LIGHT & CRISPY BEER BATTER

Yup. You guessed it. This beer batter is made to be light and crispy. We recommend preparing it just before it's fry time and whisking it every few minutes as you work to keep it well mixed. You'll notice that it is thinner than you'd expect, and that's what makes it so light and crispy. This batter is best for frying flaky white fish fillets weighing 4 to 8 ounces. That's because we've found that a fry time of 5 to 7 minutes creates a golden brown, crispy exterior. The batter tends to lose its crunch if fried for shorter times, and it tends to get too dark for our liking if fried any longer. We've also noticed that shrimp, scallops, and other shellfish are better suited to other fry styles. So when craving a classic fish-and-chips style, go for this method.

To cook, following the directions included with the Seafood Frying Chart on page 144, ready the oil for deep-frying.

Make the batter just before you are ready to begin frying to preserve the carbonation from the beer. In a large bowl, whisk together the flour, cornstarch, beer, celery salt, black pepper, garlic, onion, and cayenne (if using) until smooth.

Working with a few pieces at a time, dip the seafood into the batter, coating it generously, and carefully place the pieces directly into the hot oil. We prefer to use plating tongs or chopsticks for this step. Fry until golden brown and cooked through, turning each piece over about halfway through the cook. Immediately upon removing the pieces from the oil, season them with your choice of seasoning and serve. We find that this batter performs best with seafood that cooks in 5–7 minutes.

Makes batter for 3–5 lb seafood

1¼ cups white rice flour

1¼ cups cornstarch

1½ cups light beer

1 teaspoon celery salt

1 teaspoon freshly ground black pepper

1 teaspoon granulated garlic

1 teaspoon granulated onion

1 teaspoon cayenne pepper (optional)

3–5 lb seafood of choice

Neutral oil, for deep-frying

Seasoning of choice

PANKO CRUNCH

We like this crunchy coating best on fried shrimp, but the sky's the limit when you're in the mood for a little oomph and texture in your frying batter. In general, we think this eats best when frying seafood that cooks within 3 to 5 minutes, as that's when panko becomes golden brown and crispy. Our inspiration for the dip comes from the Chinese technique of velveting, which is essentially a quick marinade of cornstarch and egg white that is used to help give meat, poultry, and fish a tender, silky texture. We find that when the approach is applied to seafood, which typically tends to be delicate, there isn't much need for marinating, which is why we refer to the mixture as a dip. In this recipe, the dip produces a silky texture while also acting as a superior bonding agent for the panko.

To make the dip, in a large bowl, whisk together the egg whites and cornstarch until smooth. Just before you are ready to dredge and fry the seafood, put the seafood into the dip and stir gently to coat evenly.

To cook, following the directions included with the Seafood Frying Chart on page 144, ready the oil for deep-frying.

To prepare the dredge, set a large sheet pan, preferably topped with a wire rack, on your work surface. Put the panko into a large bowl. Working with a few pieces at a time, remove the seafood from the dip and drop into the panko. Bury the seafood in the panko and press down firmly to pack on the coating. Roll each piece around in the panko to ensure that all surfaces are coated, then carefully remove the seafood pieces from the panko, lightly shaking them to remove any excess panko, and place in a single layer on the rack or directly on the pan. Continue until all the seafood is dredged, making sure not to stack the coated pieces, as they may stick together.

Fry the seafood in batches as directed in the Seafood Frying Chart. Immediately upon removing the pieces from the oil, season them with your choice of seasoning and serve.

Makes breading for 3–5 lb seafood

FOR THE DIP

8 large egg whites

½ cup cornstarch

FOR THE DREDGE

4 cups panko bread crumbs

3–5 lb seafood of choice

Neutral oil, for deep-frying

Seasoning of choice

NORTH CAROLINA BONEFISH

Bonefish is regionally famous throughout coastal North Carolina, but elsewhere it is a forgotten food of Black American culture, with roots stemming from slavery. Perhaps the most well-known chef to put bonefish on the map is our good friend Ricky Moore of Saltbox Seafood Joint in Durham. A North Carolina native, Ricky grew up in the brackish town of New Bern and considers himself a seafood evangelist, making him our pastor for all things bonefish.

In coastal North Carolina, "bonefish" is an umbrella term synonymous with small freshwater and saltwater schooling fish that are caught locally throughout the year, including bluegill, butterfish, crappie, croaker, herring, hogfish, mullet, perch, porgy, spot, and whiting (aka sea mullet).

The most common way to enjoy bonefish, also called pan fish, is to dredge them with seasoned flour, panfry them whole, and serve them with Texas Pete hot sauce or apple cider vinegar and slices of soft white bread. We recommend frying these species extra hard so that even the small pinbones can be eaten without much notice, and every part of the animal, from cheek to fin, can be enjoyed.

CAJUN YUCA STEAK FRIES

Fries are a must-have at any fried fish gathering. There are tons of recipes and options for potato and sweet potato varieties, so we thought it would be nice to share a version you don't see that often. Yuca, also known as cassava or manioc, is a starchy root vegetable popular in South American, Asian, and African kitchens. It can be found at most well-stocked groceries these days. We like to make steak fries because they are an easy cut that can be done by hand. We also like how thick and hearty the fries are, and we've found the yuca holds up well, staying crispy throughout the meal.

Cut the yuca roots crosswise into segments 5–6 inches long, then peel each segment. Cut each segment in half lengthwise, then cut each half lengthwise into 4–6 wedges. Each segment should yield 8–12 steak fries measuring 5–6 inches long.

Pour oil to a depth of 4 inches into a deep fryer or deep, heavy pot and heat to 300°F. Line a large sheet pan with paper towels and set it near the stove.

When the oil is ready, working in batches to avoid crowding, carefully drop the yuca pieces into the hot oil and blanch for 3 minutes. Using a spider or other large perforated utensil, transfer to the towel-lined pan and allow to cool for 5 minutes. Repeat with the remaining yuca pieces.

Increase the oil temperature to 350°F. Again working in batches, fry the yuca pieces until they are golden brown, about 3 minutes. Scoop them out onto the towel-lined pan and immediately sprinkle with Cajun seasoning to your liking. Repeat until all the pieces are fried.

Serve the yuca fries with rémoulade and ketchup for dipping.

Makes 1 heaping basket

1–2 large pieces yuca (about 3 lb)

Neutral oil, for deep-frying

Cajun seasoning, homemade (page 240) or store-bought, for sprinkling

Rémoulade of choice (pages 241–244) and ketchup, for serving

JAMAICAN JERK TOSTONES

Crispy on the outside and tender on the inside, tostones (fried plantains) are the perfect blend of savory and sweet, making them a versatile addition to any meal. These twice-fried delights are bursting with flavor, thanks to a blend of Jamaican jerk spices that add a unique depth and heat to this cherished dish.

Pour oil to a depth of 4 inches into a deep fryer or deep, heavy pot and heat to 300°F. Line a large sheet pan with paper towels and set it near the stove.

When the oil is ready, working in two batches to avoid crowding, carefully drop the plantain pieces into the hot oil and blanch for 3 minutes. Using a spider or other large perforated utensil, transfer to the towel-lined pan and allow to cool for 5 minutes. Repeat with the remaining pieces. Smash each piece with the bottom of a skillet, making ¼-inch-thick medallions.

Increase the oil temperature to 350°F. Again working in two batches, fry the plantain medallions until they are golden brown, about 3 minutes. Scoop them out onto the towel-lined pan and immediately sprinkle with jerk seasoning to your liking. Repeat until all the pieces are fried.

Serve the tostones with rémoulade and ketchup for dipping.

Makes 8 tostones

Neutral oil, for deep-frying

2 green (unripe) plantains, peeled and each cut crosswise into 4 equal logs

Jamaican Jerk Seasoning (page 240), for sprinkling

Rémoulade of choice (pages 241–244) and ketchup, for serving

NORTH CAROLINA–STYLE HUSHPUPPIES

These savory little treats are the perfect complement to any seafood dish or backyard barbecue. Made with a combination of cornmeal, flour, spices, and just the right touch of sugar, these hushpuppies are crispy on the outside and fluffy on the inside. Serve them with your favorite dipping sauce and butter, or pile them high on a plate with some fried fish and coleslaw for a classic Southern meal. Whether you're a native North Carolinian or just looking to try something new, these crisp cornmeal balls are sure to become a staple in your recipe repertoire.

Pour oil to a depth of 4 inches into a deep fryer or deep, heavy pot and heat to 350°F. Lay a brown paper bag on a sheet pan (or line the pan with paper towels) and set it near the stove.

In a large bowl, whisk together the cornmeal, flour, sugar, baking powder, and 1 teaspoon salt. In a medium bowl, whisk together the buttermilk, butter, and egg until well blended. Pour the buttermilk mixture into the cornmeal mixture and whisk together until smooth. Pour the batter into a gallon-size resealable plastic bag.

When the oil is ready, using scissors, cut off one of the bottom corners of the plastic bag to make a hole ½ inch in diameter. Working in batches to avoid crowding, pipe 3-inch-long strips of batter into the hot oil. We like to apply constant gentle pressure while piping our hushpuppies, and we use an offset spatula or butter knife for cutting and controlling the length. They don't need to be perfectly uniform; that's part of their charm. Fry until golden brown and cooked through, about 3 minutes. Using tongs, transfer them to the lined pan to absorb excess grease and season immediately with salt to your liking. Repeat until all the batter is fried.

We like to eat these with plenty of honey, soft butter, and our homemade hot sauce.

Makes 1 heaping basket

Neutral oil, for deep-frying

2 cups fine-grind heirloom yellow cornmeal

1 cup self-rising flour

¼ cup organic sugar

1 tablespoon baking powder

Kosher salt

1¼ cups buttermilk

4 tablespoons salted butter, melted and cooled

1 large egg

Honey, room-temperature salted butter, and Sea Salt–Fermented Red Hot Sauce (page 247) or your favorite hot sauce, for serving

CAST IRON

THE FOLLOWING PAGES AIM TO DO MORE THAN just provide a wide variety of seafood dishes that celebrate the chapter's namesake. Available in skillets of all sizes, Dutch ovens, casseroles, cocottes, griddles, woks, and even a muffin pan, cast-iron cookware is truly versatile. We offer guidance on selecting the right cast iron for the job and give insights on our go-to techniques for different cooking applications, such as baking, blackening, braising, sautéing, searing, and stewing. Whether your cupboards are piled high with cast iron or you just got your first skillet to go along with this cookbook, we hope you leave this chapter with a new appreciation for this durable and adaptable cookware material.

THE SOUTHERN HERITAGE OF CAST-IRON COOKWARE

Kassady here. Growing up in South Carolina, the almighty cast-iron skillet was less a staple and more a way of life. It's what my family cooked in, fried in, baked in, and reheated in. For us, reading the words "nonstick pan" in a cookbook meant grabbing the best-seasoned skillet we had and adding a touch more grease to it than usual.

The range of cast iron my family kept was vast. A 3½-inch Lodge, a Wagner biscuit pan, and what felt like every iteration of a skillet that Griswold made hung above our kitchen island. Seasoned well, often, and beautifully, they all served their purpose, whether that was a perfect fried egg, a corn-shaped corn bread, or simply dinner made with a no. 9 skillet.

Cooking in cast iron is a time-honored tradition. Skillets are passed down from generation to generation, given as holiday and birthday gifts, and sold at antique stores. They're heirloom workhorses. Throughout the South, a dispute has inevitably risen between chefs and families alike regarding our beloved skillets: to clean with soap or not to clean with soap.

Before I was even tall enough to reach the stove, I had already been taught a few things about cast-iron cookware: don't leave a trace of water on it, wipe it down with a well-oiled towel when you're done cleaning it, and never wash cast iron with soap. To avoid soap, some cooks add kosher salt to a still-warm pan and rub the salt over the surface with a paper towel to dislodge any stuck-on bits. Others remove food remnants with a chain-mail scrubber. Still others add more fat to the still-hot pan before scrubbing it with a towel. Most of the time, though, people simply wipe out their warm skillet with a paper towel. So, to say my jaw dropped when I saw Sammy using warm, soapy water to clean the stacks of cast-iron skillets we used at our restaurant would be an understatement. From everything I had ever been taught, this was downright Southern sacrilege.

Upon further investigation, I saw that after a dip and light scrub in warm, soapy water, the skillets used to cook mac 'n' cheese and corn bread were still seasoned! He then dried them thoroughly before taking an oily towel to them—at least that part was familiar to me. "Well, I'll be damned," I said in utter disbelief.

Now I'm not here to convert anyone, but I will tell you that I have seen the light (mostly the science) behind it and would like to share what I've learned.

Not using soap on cast iron is preached as gospel because people think if you use soap, you'll strip your skillet of its seasoning. Scientifically speaking, the seasoning I'm referring to comes about through polymerization. Layers of seasoning build up every time you put fat in a cast-iron pan and cook in it at a high enough temperature. When these fats reach that high temperature, they molecularly bond to the iron and change its surface from something naturally uneven to a slick, plastic-like one. Over time, this makes the skillet nonstick and, thus, much easier to cook with. Since the fats have been polymerized, they no longer have the same properties they initially did, and so the seasoning can't be affected by dish soap.

This no-soap thinking predates the twentieth century. Back in the day, cast iron was widely used for making all types of products. Some folks even made soap in a cast-iron vessel by first boiling water and wood ash to make lye and then adding animal fat, which stripped the vessel of its seasoning. But the soap wasn't the offender; the lye was. An alkaline substance, lye breaks down organic materials, such as cast-iron seasoning. As a result, the lye thinned or fully removed the seasoning layer. Thus, a myth was born.

So, to clean with soap or not to clean with soap? That's entirely up to you. Whatever you do, please don't leave the pans wet or let them air-dry when you're done cleaning, or they're likely to rust.

CARING FOR CAST IRON

Here are some tried-and-true ways to clean your cast iron. Sometimes we use a combination of methods with really hard stuck-on messes (hello, mac 'n' cheese). No matter how you decide to clean your skillet, we can all agree on a few things: if you don't want it to rust, don't leave it wet; season it well and oil it often; and you'll never be forgiven for running it through the dishwasher. After any cleaning method, we recommend immediately oiling your cast iron (top to bottom, from handle to end) with a kitchen towel to keep it well seasoned. We prefer avocado oil, but any high-heat, neutral plant-based cooking oil will work.

For Cleaning Cast Iron

Salt Scrub
While the pan is still warm, add a small handful of kosher salt. Then, using a paper towel and firm pressure, rub out any food particles in a circular motion. Empty the remnants into a compost bin or trash can and wipe the cast iron with a clean, lint-free kitchen towel to ensure all salt particles and food bits are gone.

Warm, Soapy Water and Palm Brush
Make a batch of warm, soapy water with dish soap. Using a dish brush about the size of your palm and the soapy water, clean the food particles off of the cast iron. Wipe the cast iron down thoroughly with a clean, lint-free kitchen towel, leaving no trace of water behind.

Chain-Mail Scrubber
While the pan is still warm, using a chain-mail scrubber, apply gentle-to-firm pressure to lift off any food particles. Empty the remnants into a compost bin or trash can and wipe the cast iron with a clean, lint-free towel to ensure you've gotten everything off.

For Cleaning Enameled Cast Iron

Cleaning an enameled cast-iron pan is a little bit easier than its more rustic counterpart. You can wash it like you would a regular pan. However, those pesky black scratches won't go away with just soap, water, and elbow grease. If you want your enameled cast-iron pan (or sink) to look brand-new again, we've had great success with Bon Ami cleanser, Kohler Cast Iron, and Kohler Degreaser. And if there are any non-enameled parts to your cookware (for example, the rim of a Dutch oven), make sure you oil those parts after each cleaning the same way you would regular cast iron.

For Cleaning Rust

Lemon and Salt
Cut a lemon in half and dip the cut side in kosher salt. With firm pressure, rub vigorously over the rust spot until it lifts and you see the black of the cast iron. Wash the pan thoroughly with warm, soapy water. Dry with a clean, lint-free kitchen towel, leaving no trace of water behind. Reseason your skillet.

Steel Wool and Soapy Water
Use fine-grade steel wool and firm pressure to lift off any rust from both the inside and outside of the pan. Wash away the residue thoroughly with warm, soapy water. Dry with a clean, lint-free kitchen towel, leaving no trace of water behind. Reseason your skillet.

WHOLE SNAPPER WITH AUTUMN SUCCOTASH

Inspired by the Native American "three sisters" of corn, beans, and squash, this autumn dish pays homage to the harvest season. Hominy, lima beans, and butternut squash come together to create an Appalachian-style succotash that's hearty and flavorful. The brown butter sage adds a touch of coziness while the light and flaky snapper complements the vegetables.

Transfer the lima beans to a saucepan and add water to cover by about 2 inches and a pinch of salt. Bring to a boil over medium-high heat, adjust the heat to maintain a simmer, cover, and cook until the beans are tender, about 45 minutes. Drain and set aside.

Preheat the oven to 400°F. Score the fish twice on both sides, creating three even segments on each side. This will help the fish to cook evenly while also making it easier to eat. Season with salt and pepper and lightly drizzle with oil.

Drizzle an oval enameled cast-iron roaster with oil, place the fish in it and roast for 15 minutes. Remove the pan from the oven and carefully flip the fish, then continue roasting until fully cooked, 15–20 more minutes. It is ready when the flesh is opaque and flakes easily when tested with a knife.

While the fish roasts, fry the sage leaves. Line a plate with a few layers of paper towels and set it near the stove. In a large skillet over medium heat, melt 2 tablespoons of the butter. Lay the whole sage leaves in the pan in a single layer and panfry until the butter begins to brown and the sage becomes golden brown and aromatic, 1–2 minutes. Remove the pan from the heat and pour the contents onto the towel-lined plate. Lightly season with salt. As the leaves cool, they will become crispy.

When the fish is about 10 minutes from being done, prepare the succotash. In a saucepan over medium heat, combine the remaining 4 tablespoons butter and the stock, bring to a vigorous simmer, and cook until reduced by one-third, 3–5 minutes. Add the chopped sage, reserved lima beans, squash, and hominy and stir well. Reduce the heat to a simmer and cook, stirring frequently, until the mixture is creamy and hot, 3–5 minutes. Season with salt and pepper.

Spoon the succotash over the fish and garnish with the brown butter sage leaves, keeping some whole and crumbling others. Serve family-style.

Makes 2–4 servings

1 cup dried lima beans, picked over, then soaked overnight in water to cover, then drained and rinsed

Kosher salt and freshly ground black pepper

1 whole snapper, 2–2½ lb, dressed

Avocado oil, for drizzling and for the roaster

6 tablespoons salted butter

10–12 fresh sage leaves, plus 2 tablespoons roughly chopped

1 cup White Wine Fish Stock (page 135), or ¾ cup water mixed with ¼ cup dry white wine

1 cup peeled and diced butternut squash, cooked in lightly salted water until tender and drained

1 can (15 oz) hominy, drained and rinsed

Cast iron: oval enameled roaster

CRAWFISH & TASSO MAC 'N' CHEESE

This mac 'n' cheese offers a delightful cooking experience in a round enameled cast-iron casserole, resulting in a one-pot meal with a decadent crust that's perfect for the center of your table. While lobster mac 'n' cheese may be famous, this crawfish and tasso variation takes it up a notch with the holy trinity of celery, onion, and green chile, Cajun spice, and a Louisiana brew. Although often compared to lobster, crawfish (also known as mudbugs, crawdads, or crayfish) have a unique taste of their own. When sourcing crawfish, look for Louisiana farm-raised tail meat, a Seafood Watch Best Choice that supports small family farmers in the South.

Preheat the oven to 375°F on the convection setting or to 400°F for a conventional oven.

In a round enameled 3¼- to 4-quart cast-iron casserole over medium heat, melt the butter. Add the celery, chile, and onion and sweat, stirring frequently, until translucent, 3–5 minutes. Add the crawfish, tasso, Cajun seasoning, ale, milk, and American cheese and cook, stirring frequently, until the cheese is fully melted, 3–5 minutes.

Add the pasta and stir until evenly incorporated. The mixture will be wet, but the sauce will thicken and the pasta will absorb it as the dish bakes. Sprinkle the Cheddar cheese evenly over the top.

Bake the mac 'n' cheese until hot throughout and golden brown on top, 30–35 minutes. Let rest for 5 minutes before serving family-style directly from the casserole.

Makes 6–8 servings

4 tablespoons salted butter

½ cup diced celery

½ cup diced poblano chile

½ cup diced yellow onion

1 lb frozen Louisiana crawfish tail meat, thawed, rinsed, and drained

8 oz tasso ham, diced

1 tablespoon Cajun seasoning, homemade (page 240) or store-bought

¾ cup Abita Turbodog or other dark brown ale

¾ cup whole milk

1 lb white American cheese, chopped

1 lb dried short pasta of choice, cooked until al dente and drained

2 cups grated sharp white Cheddar cheese (about 8 oz)

Cast iron: 3¼- to 4-quart round enameled casserole

BACON & BEER BRAISED CLAMS

In one way or another, a version of this recipe has been a staple on our restaurant menus for over a decade, and for good reason. We rely on a rich combination of garlic, butter, beer, and smoky bacon to create a broth that complements the briny sweetness of the clams. The result is a bold and satisfying dish that's ideal whether you're serving a cozy dinner for two or hosting friends for an evening in. One of the most satisfying parts of this dish is dipping bread in the broth, so be sure to have plenty of crusty bread on hand.

Rinse the clams with cold water until the water runs clear, then place them in a large food container filled with ice water, making sure all the clams are submerged. Sprinkle in the cornmeal and a pinch of salt and refrigerate the clams for at least 4 hours or up to overnight. This is an old-school technique to help the clams purge any sand.

Preheat an enameled 4- to 5-quart cast-iron Dutch oven over medium heat for 3 minutes. Add the bacon, 2 tablespoons of the butter, the yellow onion, celery, bell pepper, and garlic and cook, stirring frequently, until light golden brown, about 5 minutes.

Drain and rinse the clams, discarding any that fail to close to the touch. Add the clams to the pot along with the beer and the remaining 4 tablespoons butter. Cover, raise the heat to high, and cook until the clams begin to open, 3–5 minutes. Uncover and continue cooking over high heat until the broth reduces by half and becomes rich and somewhat creamy, 4–6 minutes. Taste the broth and season with salt and black pepper to your liking. Fold in the parsley and green onions and remove from the heat.

Serve family-style directly from the Dutch oven or plated in a large serving bowl. Make sure to discard any clams that failed to open. Serve with plenty of toasted bread for dipping, and set an extra bowl on the table for discarding empty shells.

Makes 4–6 servings

3 lb clams, such as littlenecks

1 tablespoon cornmeal

Kosher salt and freshly ground black pepper

4 slices bacon, diced

6 tablespoons salted butter

½ cup diced yellow onion

½ cup diced celery

½ cup diced green bell pepper

2 tablespoons minced garlic

1 cup light golden beer, lager, or ale

¼ cup finely chopped fresh flat-leaf parsley

2 green onions, white and green parts, thinly sliced

Toasted or grilled crusty bread, for serving

Cast iron: 4- to 5-quart enameled Dutch oven

SAPELO SEA FARMS

At Sapelo Sea Farms, the clams are more than just a business; they're a way of life. Established in 1997 with a grant from the University of Georgia Marine Extension Service, this family-owned farm has been a driving force in promoting and strengthening Georgia's shellfish aquaculture industry. Today, Sapelo Sea Farms is the oldest-running clam farm in the state, producing sweet, succulent bivalves that are sought after by chefs and home cooks alike.

But what really sets Sapelo Sea Farms apart is its founder, Captain Charlie Phillips. With over forty years of experience in shrimping, fishing, and growing shellfish, Captain Charlie has a deep commitment to the well-being of our oceans and our planet. Under his leadership, Sapelo Sea Farms operates with the utmost integrity, providing delicious and sustainable shellfish while protecting the water and ecosystem in which they are farmed.

The clams themselves are grown in mesh bags on mud flats in waters adjacent to Sapelo Island, where the coastal ecosystem is ideal for producing healthy shellfish. Starting at the size of a field pea, these clams grow for almost two years before being harvested to order, cleaned, sorted by size, and sold accordingly. From Canada to South Florida, businesses along the Eastern Seaboard rely on Sapelo Sea Farms to supply them with the freshest and most flavorful clams.

In the words of Captain Charlie, growing clams is not just good for the environment and customers, it's also plain good for Georgia. So the next time you enjoy a bowl of linguine with clams or any other clam dish, remember that Sapelo Sea Farms might just be behind those clams, and it is dedicated to bringing you the best of the best.

PIN POINT HERITAGE MUSEUM

The Gullah Geechee communities of the Lowcountry coastline and Sea Islands are an extraordinary group. They are the last subset of formerly enslaved peoples to retain most of their West African culture. For hundreds of years, they've held onto their architecture, art, folklore, foodways, and pidgin language, harkening back to a time before their forced immigration.

The spirited community of Pin Point falls just outside of Savannah, Georgia, and was founded by freed slaves in 1890. Like most Gullah Geechee communities, Pin Point has considered itself "insulated, not isolated," allowing its residents to retain their vibrant heritage. Home to A.S. Varn & Son Oyster and Crab Factory, Pin Point's primary employer from 1926 to 1985, this community thrived together by harvesting, picking, and packing crab and oysters.

Today, the factory is a museum that memorializes the history of this community. During a predictably hot and humid summertime trip to Savannah, we had the pleasure of visiting the Pin Point Heritage Museum. We met with historical interpreter Gail Smith, who, as a young girl, worked an assortment of jobs at the then-operable crab factory. She led us on a tour of the museum, sharing her expert knowledge of the tools used for catching, picking, and packing crab. She taught us some words and sentences from her Gullah dialect and shared stories of her ancestors' wisdom. We bonded over our mutual appreciation of dishes like shrimp and grits, the local Carolina Gold rice, and the artist Jonathan Green. Ms. Gail was even kind enough to give us her deviled crab recipe.

The rapidly developing coastline is a concern throughout all of the coastal South, but perhaps even more so in the Gullah Geechee communities. Gullah Geechee values, social forms, and traditions are woven into the very fabric of Lowcountry culture and can be seen and felt in everything from the art and architecture to the food and language of the region. Modern influences are seeping in, and with them comes the risk of losing language, culture, and a way of life. As we continue to develop and expand our coastal communities, it's essential to remember the importance of preserving heritage and tradition. It is the duty of everyone to respect and help protect the history and legacy of the Gullah Geechee people.

GULLAH GEECHEE CRAB FRIED RICE

At the heart of Gullah Geechee cuisine are two staples deeply connected to the land and sea: Carolina Gold rice and blue crab. During the summer months, when blue crabs are abundant, you'll often find dishes like crab fried rice on tables across the Lowcountry. The ingredients celebrate the bounty of the region and pay homage to the knowledge and traditions passed down from generation to generation. Here, we rely on benne seeds (aka sesame seeds) and toasted sesame oil as bridging ingredients between Southern and Asian kitchens, and round out the umami with a touch of tamari and chile garlic paste.

Have all the ingredients for this dish close at hand so that once you start cooking, you don't need to leave the wok. Once the wok is smoking hot, this dish shouldn't take more than 5 minutes total to cook.

Using the most powerful burner on your stove, preheat a cast-iron wok over high heat for 3 minutes. If cooking on a gas range, you can remove the burner cap after the burner is lighted, for a wok range–style turbo flame. If doing so, be cautious and mindful.

Add the oil, corn, red onion, celery, bell pepper, and garlic to the wok and stir constantly using a wooden spoon, wok spatula, or comparable utensil. These aromatics should be translucent within 1 minute. Add the rice and cook, stirring frequently, for 1 minute. Add the crabmeat, tamari, benne seeds, and chile garlic sauce and stir until well incorporated. Stream in the whisked eggs around the edge of the wok along the outside of the rice mixture. The eggs should cook within 1 minute. Add the parsley and green onions and fold together all the ingredients. Taste for seasoning and adjust with salt and black pepper to your liking.

Spoon onto a serving platter and serve right away.

Makes 2–4 servings

2 tablespoons toasted sesame oil

1 cup fresh or frozen corn kernels

½ cup diced red onion

½ cup diced celery

½ cup diced red bell pepper

1 tablespoon minced garlic

4 cups day-old cooked Carolina Gold rice, refrigerated uncovered to dry out

8 oz Atlantic blue crabmeat (claw, lump, or jumbo lump), picked over for shell fragments

2 tablespoons tamari

2 tablespoons benne (sesame) seeds

1 tablespoon chile garlic sauce or paste

3 large eggs, whisked

¼ cup finely chopped fresh flat-leaf parsley

4 green onions, white and green parts, thinly sliced

Kosher salt and freshly ground black pepper

Cast iron: wok

EXTRA-FANCY CRAB CAKES

Crab cakes are a classic dish, but finding ones that truly stand out can be challenging. That's where this recipe comes in. These crab cakes are extra fancy and incredibly delicious, with a unique twist that sets them apart from the rest. The secret to their exceptional flavor and texture is the use of a classic white-fish mousseline instead of bread crumbs for binding. The mildness of the mousseline allows the delicate sweetness and texture of the crab to shine through, yielding a meaty yet tender cake. These crab cakes are perfect for a special occasion or a fancy dinner party, but they're also easy enough to make for a weekend treat. Enjoy them alongside classic Southern pairings like lightly dressed lettuces or fried green tomatoes, and be sure to serve them with lemon and rémoulade.

In a food processor, combine the fish, egg white, and cream. Working quickly to keep the mixture cold, process until smooth. This is the mousseline that will bind the cakes.

Transfer the mousseline to a bowl and add the crabmeat, parsley, green onions, and 1/2 teaspoon each salt and pepper. Fold everything together with a rubber spatula until well mixed. Divide the mixture into 6 equal portions. Each should weigh about 4 oz. Shape each portion into a cake 3 inches in diameter and 1 inch thick.

Preheat a cast-iron griddle over medium heat for 5 minutes. Meanwhile, in a small saucepan, melt the butter over low heat. Set it aside off the heat along with a basting brush.

Lightly season both sides of each crab cake with salt and pepper. Spread the oil evenly across the griddle and place the crab cakes on the griddle. Sear until golden brown on the first side, 3–4 minutes. Carefully flip the cakes, then begin basting them with the melted butter. Sear the second side, basting several times throughout the cooking, until golden brown, 3–4 minutes. The cakes are done when an instant-read thermometer inserted into the center of a cake registers 160°F.

Transfer the cakes to a serving plate and serve right away, accompanied with lemon wedges and rémoulade.

Makes 6 crab cakes

8 oz mild white fish, such as grouper, cobia, hake, cod, or snapper, diced and kept cold

1 large egg white, kept cold

1/4 cup cold heavy cream

8 oz Atlantic blue crabmeat (claw, lump, or jumbo lump), picked over for shell fragments and gently squeezed to remove excess liquid

1/4 cup finely chopped fresh flat-leaf parsley

2 green onions, white and green parts, thinly sliced

Kosher salt and freshly ground black pepper

4 tablespoons salted butter

2 tablespoons avocado oil

Lemon wedges and rémoulade of choice (pages 241–244), for serving

Cast iron: griddle

Note: Basting in butter halfway through the cook is key, and given this chapter is all about celebrating blacksmiths, we're proudly recommending y'all get yourself a chain-mail sop mop from Georgia-based Sea Island Forge.

CRAB GRATIN EN COCOTTE WITH CAJUN FRIED SALTINES

This dish exemplifies the beauty of culinary simplicity. With just a handful of ingredients, you can create a delicious and satisfying side or snack that celebrates the flavors of the sea. While the crab and cheese are certainly the stars of the show, the Cajun-seasoned fried saltines are not to be overlooked, as they play a crucial role in making this dish a true feast for the senses. The crispy, slightly spicy crackers complement the rich, creamy gratin and add a wonderful crunch and depth of flavor to the dish.

Preheat the oven to 375°F.

In a bowl, combine the crabmeat, 1/2 cup of the Cheddar, the cream, green onion (if using), garlic, salt, and pepper and mix well. Pour the mixture into a 3 1/2- to 4-cup cast-iron cocotte (or 6-inch cast-iron skillet) and top evenly with the remaining 1 cup Cheddar.

Bake the gratin until hot, bubbly, and golden brown, 20–25 minutes. Enjoy immediately with the fried saltines.

...

Cajun Fried Saltines
Makes about 40 crackers

Neutral oil, for deep-frying
1 sleeve saltine crackers
2 teaspoons Cajun seasoning, homemade (page 240) or store-bought

Pour oil to a depth of 4 inches into a deep fryer or deep, heavy pot and heat to 350°F.

When the oil is ready, add half of the crackers and fry, carefully stirring with a metal spoon to ensure even cooking, for 1–2 minutes. They will turn golden. If using a deep fryer, drain the crackers well in the fryer basket, then transfer them to a bowl. If using a pot, scoop the crackers out with a spider or other large perforated utensil, draining them well over the pot, and then transfer them to a bowl. Season immediately with half of the seasoning. Repeat with the remaining crackers and seasoning.

These crackers are great served warm but can also be made ahead of time. Once cool, they can be packed into an airtight food storage container and kept in the pantry for up to 2 weeks.

Makes 2–4 servings

8 oz Atlantic blue crabmeat (claw, lump, or jumbo lump), picked over for shell fragments and gently squeezed to remove excess liquid

1 1/2 cups grated sharp white Cheddar cheese (about 6 oz)

1/4 cup heavy cream

2 green onions, white and green parts, thinly sliced (optional)

1/4 teaspoon granulated garlic

1/4 teaspoon kosher salt

1/4 teaspoon freshly ground black pepper

Cajun Fried Saltines, crackers, or toast, for serving

Cast iron: 3 1/2- to 4-cup cocotte

MAHI-MAHI CURRY POT

This fish curry is a flavorful tribute to the vibrant culinary traditions of the Caribbean, with inspiration stemming from the curries of Jamaica, Trinidad, and Tobago. The succulent meat of the mahi-mahi combined with a variety of hearty vegetables results in a warming and soul-satisfying dish that's just as comforting as it is tropical. Top with cilantro and a squeeze of fresh lime juice for a bright finish reminiscent of the islands. Not only does this one-pot dish boast a mouthwatering flavor profile, but it also comes together in under an hour.

In a 5- to 7-quart cast-iron Dutch oven over medium heat, melt the coconut oil. Add the onion, ginger, chile, and garlic and sweat, stirring frequently, until translucent, 3–5 minutes. Add the carrots, yam, and plantain and continue sweating the mixture, stirring somewhat frequently, for 2–3 minutes. Add the sugar, vanilla, 1 teaspoon of the jerk seasoning, and enough coconut milk to cover and bring to a simmer. Reduce the heat to maintain a gentle simmer. Taste for seasoning and adjust with salt and pepper to your liking. Cover and gently simmer until the carrots are tender, 25–30 minutes.

To finish, season the fish pieces on both sides with the remaining 1 teaspoon jerk seasoning and gently place them in the pot, submerging each piece about two-thirds of the way into the curry. Re-cover the pot and poach the fish until fully cooked, 3–5 minutes.

We love to serve this curry family-style, landing the Dutch oven on a trivet at the center of the table. We place a small bowl of cilantro and another of lime wedges and a big bowl of freshly steamed rice on the table for diners to help themselves.

Makes 2–4 servings

1/4 cup coconut oil

1/2 yellow onion, diced

1/4 cup peeled and minced fresh ginger

1 poblano chile, diced

2 tablespoons minced garlic

3 carrots, peeled and diced

1 large yam, peeled and diced

1 green (unripe) plantain, peeled and diced

1 tablespoon coconut sugar or firmly packed light brown sugar

1/2 teaspoon pure vanilla extract

2 teaspoons Jamaican Jerk Seasoning (page 240)

3 1/4–4 cups coconut milk

Kosher salt and freshly ground black pepper

1 lb mahi-mahi fillet, cut into 1 1/2-inch pieces

Chopped fresh cilantro and lime wedges, for serving

Hot steamed Carolina Gold rice, for serving

Cast iron: 5- to 7-quart Dutch oven

SMITHEY IRONWARE

Cast-iron cookware has a long and fascinating history in the United States. In the nineteenth century, foundries in Pennsylvania, Ohio, and Tennessee produced a wide range of cast-iron cooking vessels, from skillets to Dutch ovens. Companies such as Griswold, Wagner, and Lodge became household names, and their products were known for their high quality and durability.

However, the rise of nonstick Teflon technology in the mid-twentieth century had a significant impact on the cast-iron cookware industry. Nonstick pans were lighter and less expensive, and many consumers opted for this new technology over traditional cast iron. As a result, some cast-iron foundries struggled, and the quality and reputation of cast-iron cookware declined. Beloved companies, such as Griswold and Wagner, which had already been struggling throughout the Great Depression, could not survive the low demand caused by the newfound popularity of Teflon. Lodge also felt the impact of this shift in consumer preferences, but the company adapted by expanding its product line to include enamel-coated cast-iron cookware and other products. Over the years, Griswold and Wagner were both bought and sold numerous times, and all of that trading affected their quality and reputation. Today, any serious collector disregards pans forged by those two icons past the 1950s.

Despite this history, there has been a resurgence of interest in cast-iron cookware in recent years. Companies like Smithey Ironware have emerged, and they're doing it right. We discovered Smithey when our friend and host of the *Southern Fork* podcast Stephanie Burt generously gifted us a no. 12 griddle. Impressed after the first use, we're still hooked and singing the praises of Smithey.

Based in Charleston, South Carolina, Smithey Ironware stands out in the world of cookware for its commitment to producing high-quality, premium cast-iron and carbon-steel cookware that is both functional and beautiful. The company has a team of designers, engineers, foundry workers, metal grinders, craftspeople, and seasoners who work together to create products that meet its high standards. One of the things that sets Smithey apart is its unique manufacturing process, which involves grinding the inside of the pan to make it smooth and lustrous. This process results in cookware that performs exceptionally well.

Another important aspect of Smithey is its commitment to sustainability and ethical production practices. The company uses recycled materials whenever possible and works with foundries that are committed to reducing waste and minimizing their impact on the environment. Smithey's cookware—from skillets and Dutch ovens to grill pans and roasters—is suitable for home cooks at all levels. It is an excellent choice for anyone who is passionate about cooking with top-notch tools and wants to invest in a piece of cookware that will last for generations. The company encourages its customers to use its cookware often, and well.

PERFECTLY BLACKENED FISH

In these parts, we are blessed with an abundance of delicious fish species that are just begging to be blackened. Our top picks include bass, catfish, cobia, drum, grouper, mahi-mahi, mullet, redfish, sheepshead, snapper, tilefish, triggerfish, wahoo, and wreckfish. To achieve a perfectly blackened fish, we suggest starting with a 5- to 6-ounce portion of meaty white-flesh fish. This type of fish is easier to handle when flipping, and by the time blackening is achieved on all sides, it tends to be cooked evenly throughout. Using a no. 12 skillet, which measures about 12 inches in diameter, is essential to ensure you have plenty of room to flip and maintain heat efficiently. It will also help you avoid the common pitfalls of under- or overblackening and cooking. When it comes to the cooking process, the key is to put the dry-spiced piece of fish into a skillet with hot oil. This allows the fish to blacken properly without sticking, resulting in a perfectly blackened piece of fish with just the right amount of crunch.

We often find ourselves serving blackened fish atop a heaping bowl of Coconut Ginger Collards (page 235). It's a healthy, hearty, and soul-satisfying meal that hits the spot on a Tuesday night and for Sunday supper alike. Add a fried egg and you're ready to brunch.

Place a large sheet pan, preferably topped with a wire rack, next to the stove. Preheat a no. 12 cast-iron skillet over medium heat for 5 minutes. While the pan heats, place the fish on paper towels, cover with more paper towels, and pat dry to remove excess moisture. Spread the Cajun seasoning on a small, flat plate, then coat each piece of fish on all sides with the seasoning.

When the pan is smoking hot, pour the oil into the pan. Carefully place each piece of fish into the pan. Turn the heat up to medium-high and sear each side, flipping the pieces once, until well blackened, 2–3 minutes per side. If the fish appears to have a third side, blacken that too. We find it critical to use a fish spatula (see sidebar) for this technique, and for cooking any piece of fish in a skillet, for that matter.

Once the fish is fully blackened, arrange it in a single layer on the rack or directly on the pan and let rest for 3 minutes before serving.

Makes 2–4 servings

2–4 pieces meaty white fish fillet, 5–6 oz each

½ cup Cajun seasoning, homemade (page 240) or store-bought

¼ cup avocado oil

Cast iron: no. 12 skillet

Fish Spatulas

Whether you're a professional chef or a home cook, a good fish spatula is a must-have tool for your kitchen. It is not only essential for flipping delicate fish fillets but also for a variety of other flipping tasks, such as burgers, tortillas, grilled cheese, and even eggs.

When it comes to choosing the right fish spatula for your kitchen, a few brands stand out. Smithey Ironware (page 180) is a great option for those who frequently use cast-iron pans, as its spatulas are specially designed for this type of cooking. The Mercer Culinary Hell's Tools high-temperature slotted turner is a versatile tool that's also safe to use with nonstick finishes and comes in a wide range of colors. And for those who love outdoor cooking, Toadfish makes its "Ultimate" spatula with both durability and function in mind, featuring full stainless-steel construction and an ultra-thin flexible tip.

SAVORY OYSTER BREAD PUDDING

Elevate your next holiday feast or weekend brunch with this decadent oyster bread pudding. Creamy and indulgent, this dish combines oysters with a hearty bread base, resulting in a melt-in-your-mouth texture and rich, savory flavor. For Mother's Day, we enjoy serving each portion smothered in béarnaise sauce and topped with crispy country ham and a poached egg—a Southern riff on eggs Benedict.

In a skillet over medium heat, melt the butter. Add the onion, celery, chile, and garlic and sweat, stirring frequently, until translucent, 4–5 minutes. Transfer to a small dish and refrigerate until well chilled.

In a large bowl, combine the oysters, challah, milk, eggs, salt, pepper, and chilled onion mixture and fold together with your hands until evenly mixed. Pack the mixture into an airtight food storage container, making sure all the bread is submerged in liquid, and refrigerate overnight.

The next day, preheat the oven to 400°F. Grease a 12-cup cast-iron muffin pan with butter.

Evenly distribute the pudding mixture among the prepared muffin cups, filling each one about two-thirds full. Bake until golden brown and an instant-read thermometer inserted into the center of a pudding registers 165°F, 35–40 minutes. Let rest in the pan on a wire rack for 10 minutes, then unmold and serve warm.

Makes 10–12 servings

2 tablespoons salted butter, plus more for greasing the pan

½ yellow onion, diced

2 celery ribs, diced

½ poblano chile, diced

1 tablespoon minced garlic

1 lb freshly shucked frying oysters with liquor, roughly chopped

8 cups torn challah, in 1- to 3-inch pieces (about ¾ loaf)

1 cup whole milk

2 large eggs, whisked

1 teaspoon kosher salt

½ teaspoon freshly ground black pepper

Cast iron: 12-cup muffin pan

SMOKED TROUT & SWEET POTATO HASH

Elevate your brunch game with this inspired hash. It's a dish that's sure to impress any time of day, but it's during cozy autumn gatherings that this flavorful hash really shines as the centerpiece of a menu. The smokiness of the trout, the heartiness of the sweet potatoes, and the subtle sweetness of maple are perfectly balanced by the savory notes of rosemary. It's the ultimate comfort food that's just as good for breakfast as it is for dinner. We like to use smoked trout fillets from Sunburst Trout Farms, a North Carolina family-run business that dates back to the late 1940s.

Preheat the oven to 400ºF.

Preheat a 14-inch dual-handle cast-iron skillet over medium heat for 3 minutes. When the pan is hot, add the oil and then add the sweet potatoes and onion and cook, stirring somewhat frequently, until the onion is translucent, 3–5 minutes. Lightly season with salt and pepper, add 2 tablespoons of the butter, and continue to stir somewhat frequently until the sweet potatoes are almost fully cooked, 12–15 minutes. Add the trout, maple syrup, rosemary, and the remaining 2 tablespoons butter and stir until fully incorporated. Taste the hash and season with salt and pepper to your liking.

Using the back of a spoon, make indents in the hash for the eggs, then crack an egg into each nook. Place the skillet in the oven and bake for 5 minutes. This will yield fully set whites with runny yolks for dipping. Enjoy right away directly from the pan with toast.

Makes 2–4 servings

2 tablespoons avocado oil

1–2 sweet potatoes, depending on the number of servings, peeled and diced

1 Vidalia or other sweet onion, diced

Kosher salt and freshly ground black pepper

4 tablespoons salted butter

1 lb smoked trout fillets, skinned and diced

2 tablespoons pure maple syrup

2 tablespoons chopped fresh rosemary leaves

4–8 large eggs, depending on the number of servings

Toast, for serving

Cast iron: 14-inch dual-handle skillet

SEARED SEA SCALLOPS WITH MIDDLINS

If you're already a fan of scallops and risotto, you're in for a real treat with this recipe. Rice middlins are a by-product of Carolina Gold rice, the beloved heirloom rice that has been a staple of Southern cuisine for generations. Historically speaking, these broken or imperfect rice grains were not suitable for trade or export, so they found a special place in the hearts and kitchens of Lowcountry cooks, who used them in breads, porridges, and other dishes. With their nutty, floral flavor profile and all the pedigree of Carolina Gold, rice middlins are a true gem of the Southern larder.

In a deep 9-inch cast-iron skillet over medium heat, melt 1 tablespoon of the butter. Add the yellow onion, celery, bell pepper, and garlic and sweat, stirring frequently, until translucent, 3–5 minutes. Add the rice middlins and toast, stirring frequently, for 1 minute. Add the wine and cook, stirring frequently, until absorbed. Reduce the heat to medium-low. Add about 1½ cups of the stock and cook, stirring frequently, until the stock is absorbed by the rice. Continue adding the stock in roughly 1½-cup increments, just as you would if making risotto, until the rice is al dente.

When the rice is about halfway through cooking, preheat a cast-iron griddle over medium-high heat for 3 minutes. While the griddle heats, remove the foot muscle from the side of each scallop, then place the scallops on paper towels, cover with more paper towels, and pat dry to remove excess moisture. Lightly season the scallops on all sides with salt. When the griddle is ready, carefully pour just enough oil onto the surface to coat lightly, then place the scallops on the griddle. Sear until a rich golden brown starts to form on the first side, 2–3 minutes. Then, working quickly, add 1 tablespoon of the butter to the griddle and allow to brown. Continue cooking the first side of the scallops until a deep golden brown crust forms, 1–2 minutes longer. Flip each scallop and turn off the heat. Allow the scallops to continue cooking on the griddle for 2–3 minutes longer, then transfer to a plate and let rest.

If you've timed everything well, the rice has just become al dente and is ready to finish. Add the remaining 2 tablespoons butter, the parsley, and the green onions to the middlins and stir until incorporated. Season with salt and black pepper.

Divide the middlins between bowls, scatter the scallops on top, and garnish with a lemon wedge, celery leaves, and more black pepper. Serve right away.

Makes 2 servings

4 tablespoons salted butter

½ cup diced yellow onion

½ cup diced celery

½ cup diced green bell pepper

1 tablespoon minced garlic

1 cup Carolina Gold rice middlins

½ cup dry white wine

4–6 cups fish stock, homemade (page 135) or store-bought

1 lb diver-caught sea scallops

Kosher salt and freshly ground black pepper

Avocado oil, for cooking

¼ cup finely chopped fresh flat-leaf parsley

2 green onions, white and green parts, thinly sliced

2 lemon wedges and fresh celery leaves, for garnish

Cast iron: deep 12-inch skillet and griddle

HARDWOOD

THERE'S UNDOUBTEDLY SOMETHING SPECIAL, MAYBE even spiritual, about cooking with hardwood—the fire, the aroma, the romance. We can't get enough. Many home cooks and chefs avoid cooking over a hardwood fire, intimidated by its requirements for skill and experience. That's why we've decided to offer this chapter, which is somewhat of a crash course. It showcases a dynamic range of backyard cookery that will help you hone a variety of cooking skills while eating damn well.

Today, there's an abundance of equipment, tools, and techniques that people can employ to sharpen their hardwood cooking skills. For us, it all starts with the simplicity of grilling over a mixture of natural lump charcoal and hardwood split logs. With that in mind, we have created hardwood recipes for cooks of any skill level and any backyard rig, from old-school Smokey Joe to Santa Maria–style cowboy pit to cast-iron fire kettle. Of course, human ingenuity has provided us with what seems to be an endless array of hardwood-fueled cooking devices, so we'll also highlight the dynamic range of cooking that can be performed on pellet grills and in wood-fired ovens. In Hardwood, you'll find a smoke-filled look at some of our favorite methods and wood types for preparing seafood dishes.

MASTERING HARDWOOD COOKERY

Through cooking intuitively and intentionally, you'll learn to master your tools and equipment over time. We encourage you to experiment with different blends of charcoal and hardwood. We often cook with hickory for its distinctly sweet and tangy Southern barbecue notes, but we keep an assortment of other hardwoods on hand, including alder, apple, cherry, mesquite, peach, and pecan. We think you'll be pleasantly surprised by how quickly you can get good at cooking with hardwood. By sharing our key principles and techniques, we'll give you the guidance needed to start perfecting your own style of hardwood cookery.

Hardwood

It all boils (or burns) down to good wood. Whether it be hickory, mesquite, peach, or pecan (to name a few), it's the flavor of the smoke and the meticulous maintenance of the burn that make the dish. Determine the hard-lump natural charcoal and hardwood(s) that you feel lend the best flavor(s) to your cooking. Make sure you can source them locally and consistently. When it comes to getting really good at any method of cooking, there needs to be a common set of factors involved.

Equipment

If you don't have any outdoor cooking equipment that lends itself to hardwood cooking, you'll need to go shopping. We've taken our time to create our dream outdoor kitchen, and we recommend that you take your time as well. Invest in equipment that has an excellent reputation for performance and can withstand the elements of your particular region. From our perspective, there are three main categories of outdoor hardwood cooking equipment: charcoal grill, wood-fired oven, and pellet grill. Throughout this chapter, we offer guidance for cooking and purchasing from all three categories. Although we don't regularly cook on one ourselves, if you're looking for something more entry-level, we recommend the Weber Smokey Joe. Over the years, it has made a good name for itself as a backyard standard, and it is perhaps the most approachable, affordable, and dependable option on the market. Use an infrared thermometer to test for temperature and determine heat zones. Hardwood cooking is far from elite, and we wouldn't want anyone with a passion for gaining this skill set to be held back by access. We've cooked on rusted-out, twenty-year-old Smokey Joes enough times to say that this Weber bestseller has been labeled the backyard go-to for good reason.

Lifestyle

Take the time to create an enjoyable lifestyle area around your outdoor grilling space. Cooking shouldn't feel like a chore. Make sure you can sit down and enjoy a cold drink with friends and family throughout the cooking process. That's always best, of course, but we find that it is especially true when cooking with hardwood, as the fire provides a sense of old-fashioned togetherness like nothing else.

Practice

Practice makes perfect. We guarantee that if you follow our steps and guidance, and challenge yourself to cook with hardwood for ten days straight, you'll have gained the intuition, experience, and confidence that would otherwise have taken years to acquire.

HARDWOOD GRILLING

Hardwood grilling requires a bit more time and expertise than modern-day gas grilling. However, the flavors and textures that result from hardwood grilling are generally regarded as superior, and the method itself can be more rewarding in the most primal sense. When cooking with hardwood, we prefer to work with a combination of natural hardwood lump charcoal and grilling wood, either in the form of split logs or wood chunks. Wood chips can be used to infuse variety-specific smoke flavoring, but they burn fast and offer little to no actual cooking power, which is why we don't call for them here.

To prepare your heat source, start by filling a charcoal chimney with natural hardwood lump charcoal. Place the chimney on your outdoor grilling apparatus with a natural tumbleweed fire starter underneath, light the fire starter, and let the charcoal heat through, which should take 10 to 12 minutes. You'll know your charcoal is ready when it's glowing red and a jet-like flame is shooting from the center of the chimney. Working with caution, and preferably wearing a protective glove to prevent burns, carefully pour the hot coals into the center of your grilling apparatus. Arrange three to four pieces of split-log hardwood or six to eight pieces of wood chunks around the perimeter of the charcoal. Use a poker or long grilling tongs to set the wood into the charcoal, ensuring that it's in direct contact with the hot coals. Allow the wood to heat until it is strongly burning, which should take between 12 and 15 minutes. From here, you're ready to cook. To recap, the entire process of getting your heat source and grill ready for cooking should take about 30 minutes.

We find that this is enough fuel to provide strong, even cooking for up to 45 minutes, which is ample for any of our recipes and for most other high-heat direct-cooking recipes we can think of. If you're planning for longer cooking sessions, add a few pieces of hardwood when the heat source begins to temper down to medium heat. Letting it drop any lower will produce inconsistencies in the cooking process, which can result in foods drying out. When it comes to hardwood cooking, most folks are concerned about burning their food. But the more likely problem is overcooking because a fire is not hot enough, which causes an unnecessarily long cook.

Use a poker or long grilling tongs to move your fuel around as it burns down. This will help maintain an even oven of hot coals. Be attentive to where your hot spots are, and place food on your grill according to the desired heat levels. We like to start out by placing food on a high-heat area to achieve seared grill marks quickly. Pay close attention as the color goes from deep golden brown to black. This indicates rich flavor from the caramelization of sugar and the Maillard reaction of protein. Keep in mind that when the exterior of your food reaches such high temperatures, it can go from benevolent to burnt quickly. So once you get this color, it's critical to keep moving your food, whether that means you flip it, rotate it, or move it to a lower-temperature area. If you're fortunate enough to have a grill with a height-adjustable grill grate, you can simply raise the grate, instantly adjusting the distance between the food and the fuel and thus lowering the heat.

HICKORY-ROASTED MONKFISH VERACRUZANA

Monkfish is known for its mild, slightly sweet, and firm flesh that is often compared to lobster. In the United States, it is sustainably managed and responsibly wild caught year-round from Maine to North Carolina. In terms of flavor, texture, muscle structure, and cooking dynamic, monkfish is one of the most unique seafood species on the market. It cooks and eats more like a piece of terrestrial protein than it does a finfish, and given the fillets are similar in shape and size to a pork tenderloin, we like to treat this fish like we would pork.

Monkfish loins are covered in a bluish-gray membrane, which must be removed before cooking. If left on, the membrane will cause the loin to shrink and curl during cooking, yielding a tough, chewy result. Removing it is exactly like removing silver skin from pork, beef, or lamb: using a fillet or similar knife, thoughtfully trim off the membrane, being careful not to cut into the flesh.

In a bowl, combine the monkfish, oil, lemon zest and juice, and garlic, gently season with salt and pepper, and turn the monkfish to coat evenly. Cover and marinate in the refrigerator for at least 1 hour or up to 4 hours.

While the fish marinates, make the salsa. In a bowl, combine the tomatoes, olives, red peppers, parsley, green onions, garlic, chile (if using), oil, vinegar, and paprika and stir gently to mix well. Season with salt and black pepper and set aside.

To cook the fish, prepare a fire in your fire kettle or charcoal grill using split-log hickory according to our Hardwood Grilling instructions on page 193. Once the fire is ready for cooking, remove the monkfish from the marinade and place on a high-heat area of the grill. We typically treat monkfish loin as having three sides, as it's a round loin that resembles a pork tenderloin. We cook each of the three sides to a deep golden brown before flipping, and have found that each side cooks for 4–6 minutes, with the total cook time 12–18 minutes. Given the shape of the loins, we rest them on a wire rack set atop a sheet pan for 7–10 minutes, just as we would a loin of terrestrial protein.

To serve, slice the loins on the diagonal into roughly 3/4-inch-thick pieces. Shingle the pieces across a serving plate and accompany with the salsa.

Makes 2–4 servings

2 monkfish loins, about 12 oz each

1/4 cup extra-virgin olive oil

Grated zest and juice of 1 lemon

2 cloves garlic, finely grated with a zester

Kosher salt and freshly ground black pepper

FOR THE SALSA

1 cup finely chopped tomatoes

1 cup pitted and chopped Castelvetrano olives

1 cup finely chopped fire-roasted red sweet peppers

1/4 cup finely chopped fresh flat-leaf parsley

2 green onions, white and green parts, thinly sliced

3 cloves garlic, finely grated with a zester

2 tablespoons crushed Calabrian chile (optional)

1/4 cup extra-virgin olive oil

1 tablespoon sherry vinegar

1 teaspoon smoked paprika

Kosher salt and freshly ground black pepper

HARISSA CHARRED CATFISH

Catfish have a slightly sweet, mild flavor and dense, moist flesh. This bottom-feeding species is notorious for having a muddy flavor. It is not because the fish are actually eating mud, which causes folks to conclude that catfish are a dirty species, but rather an organic result of algae and microorganisms found in freshwater. We've discovered that the best way to avoid the funky flavor is to source US sustainably farmed fish.

Catfish are an incredible species for farm raising. They grow fast, eat a wide variety of plants and animals, and yield large meaty fillets. Consequently, catfish can endure rather poor living conditions, and the unfortunate result is that there are quite literally tons of unsustainably farmed catfish on the US market.

With that being said, we urge you to keep an open mind toward aquaculture, because when it's done right, it's an incredible method for raising delicious, healthy fish and shellfish. In general, the best thing you can do to guarantee you're getting high quality is to purchase a US product, be it farm raised or wild caught. When it comes to fish and shellfish, the United States has the highest standards and strictest science-based regulations in the world. Unfortunately, 90 percent of the fish and shellfish eaten in the United States is imported.

We've found that the cleanest, healthiest, and best-tasting catfish come from Mississippi and are farm raised. Catfish has been a staple on our menus for years, and we've actually garnered regulars due to its superior taste.

For this recipe, we prefer catfish for its rich, meaty texture, which holds up well over hardwood cooking and stands up to the bold flavors of our harissa ketchup, which we slather on for added depth and caramelization. This preparation also works well with grouper, cobia, or mahi-mahi fillets.

At the table, we brighten things up with a refreshing mix of fennel, mint, and lemon, which gives this dish some coastal Levantine vibes. We generally round out the menu with lightly dressed lettuces and a simple potato preparation—roasted, fried, or even in salad form.

Makes 2–4 servings

FOR THE HARISSA KETCHUP

½ cup canned tomato paste

¼ cup water

1 tablespoon extra-virgin olive oil

Grated zest and juice of 1 lime

1 clove garlic, finely grated with a zester

2 tablespoons dry harissa seasoning

1 teaspoon kosher salt

—

2–4 catfish fillets, about 8 oz each

Extra-virgin olive oil, for rubbing on fish

2 tablespoons Carolina Reaper Harissa (page 241)

Kosher salt and freshly ground black pepper

1 fennel bulb, trimmed and shaved

Leaves from ½ bunch fresh mint

Grated zest and juice of ½ lemon

First, prepare the harissa ketchup. In a bowl, whisk together all the ingredients until well mixed. It is ready to use and imparts the best flavor at room temperature. It can be made up to 2 weeks in advance and stored in an airtight container in the refrigerator, then left to temper at room temperature for 1 hour before using.

To cook the fish, prepare a fire in your fire kettle or charcoal grill according to our Hardwood Grilling instructions on page 193. While the fire heats, lightly rub the fillets on both sides with oil and season on both sides with the Carolina Reaper Harissa and with salt and pepper.

Slather the fillets with the harissa ketchup before placing them on the center of the grill grate, then cook, turning once, until caramelized and charred, about 4 minutes on each side.

When the fish is done, allow it to rest for 5 minutes. While it rests, in a bowl, combine the fennel, mint, and lemon zest and juice. Lightly season with salt and pepper and gently mix.

To serve family-style, place the fillets on a serving plate and top with the fennel-mint mixture.

Harissa

Sammy here. My Lebanese heritage and my childhood memories of the cooking of my *taita* (grandmother) often influence my cuisine, and I find that the bold and zesty flavors of harissa blend seamlessly into the Southern kitchen.

Harissa is a linchpin throughout the cuisines of North Africa and in parts of the Middle East. It is prepared as both a dry seasoning and a wet, saucy paste, and although its character is often quite complex, at its core, it is simply salt, dried chiles, and olive oil (for the paste). When comparing harissa recipes, what distinguishes one from another is usually the type of chiles used. Smoked Spanish paprika provides body and texture, and I rely on it heavily in my harissa variations. Our recipes for dry harissa seasoning (page 241) and harissa paste (aka harissa ketchup, opposite) illustrate that cuisine is never fixed but rather is something that continues to evolve generationally.

Oftentimes, we find ourselves substituting our dry seasoning in recipes that would typically go great with Cajun seasoning, from blackened redfish to popcorn shrimp. Our harissa paste is extremely versatile and is a delicious accompaniment for fried fish and French fries alike, but don't stop there. Smear it on an oyster po'boy or splash some into your scrambled eggs for a fiery kick.

CAROLINA GOLD BARBECUED GROUPER CHEEKS

Groupers—including black, gag, and red—are a dependable set of species to source, as they're wild caught throughout the South Atlantic, Gulf of Mexico, and US Caribbean year-round. With a firm and flaky texture and mild flavor, grouper is uniquely delicious and is often described as being a cross between halibut and bass. Groupers are quite large and can range from fifty to one hundred pounds, yielding massive fillets and collar cuts—and cheek meat similar in size to hog jowls.

Here, we treat the grouper cheeks as if we were preparing barbecued pork—like the good Carolinians that we are. Although they cook up much quicker than hog meat, their muscle structure provides enough firmness for you to slather on barbecue sauce and char hard over hickory or other wood without overcooking. The result is a sweet, smoky, tangy, crispy goodness that will have your taste buds dancing. We think that serving these cheeks with our Pop's Slaw is an absolute must.

Prepare a fire in your fire kettle or charcoal grill according to our Hardwood Grilling instructions on page 193. While the fire heats, slather both sides of the grouper cheeks with the BBQ sauce and place on a sheet pan. Gently season on both sides with salt and pepper.

Once the heat source is roaring and the grill surface registers between 400° and 500°F, lightly brush or mist the grill grate with oil. Place the grouper on the grate and cook, turning once, until deep golden brown on both sides, 5–7 minutes on each side. Be cautious when flipping, as sticking sometimes occurs. We use our fish spatula (page 183) here, and before we flip, we scrape underneath the fish from all sides to ensure we've removed it from any stuck points on the grate.

When the fish is done, allow it to rest for 5 minutes. We enjoy serving the grouper cheeks in a truly Southern way, and that means with our Pop's Slaw. But from there, the sky's the limit.

Makes 2–4 servings

4 grouper cheeks or fillets, 5–6 oz each

Carolina Gold BBQ Sauce (page 245), for slathering

Kosher salt and freshly ground black pepper

Avocado oil, for the grill

Pop's Slaw (page 238), for serving

WRECKFISH À LA PARRILLA

Wreckfish is mild and meaty, with a flavor and texture often compared to grouper or swordfish. Sourcing it can be somewhat challenging, as its market availability is sporadic due to several factors, including seasonality, demand, locale, and a limited number of fishermen. The only true wreckfish fishery in the United States is in the Charleston Bump, a deepwater bank off South Carolina and Georgia. This complex habitat features a series of rocky cliffs, overhangs, corals, and steep scarps undercut with extensive caves. In these caves, huge predatory wreckfish can grow up to one hundred pounds.

Wreckfish is one of the most unique and delicious species of finfish we've ever eaten, and we highly recommend doing what you can to get some into your kitchen. Here, we lean into its meatiness and prepare it in a style inspired by Spanish wood-fired grilling. Our savory Southern riff on a sweet-pepper romesco sauce features charred Anaheim chiles and onions along with peanuts and benne seeds. Our Cajun version of dukkah incorporates another layer of peanuts and benne seeds, adding texture and Moroccan gusto. The result is a dish that is simple and rustic yet deeply complex and beautiful. If you can't get your hands on wreckfish, don't let that hold you back from enjoying this recipe. It's wonderful with swordfish, grouper, or cobia too. As with most of our Mediterranean-inspired fish preparations, we like to serve the fish with a lightly dressed green salad and roasted or fried potatoes.

To make the dukkah, in a food processor, combine the peanuts, benne seeds, and Cajun seasoning and process until crumbly and somewhat sticky, about 1 minute. Set the dukkah aside.

To prepare the romesco and fish, start by preparing a fire in your fire kettle or charcoal grill according to our Hardwood Grilling instructions on page 193. While the fire heats, lightly rub the chiles and onion slices for the romesco and the fish fillets on both sides with oil and then lightly season both sides with salt and pepper.

Once the heat source is roaring and the grill surface registers between 400° and 500°F, lightly brush or mist the grill grate with avocado oil. Place the chiles and onion slices on the grate and cook, turning once, until deeply charred on both sides, 5–8 minutes on each side. Transfer to an airtight food storage container, seal closed, and let steam for 5 minutes.

Makes 2–4 servings

FOR THE CAJUN DUKKAH

½ cup lightly salted or unsalted dry-roasted peanuts

¼ cup benne (sesame) seeds

2 tablespoons Cajun seasoning, homemade (page 240) or store-bought

FOR THE ROMESCO

2 Anaheim or poblano chiles, halved lengthwise

1 Vidalia or other sweet onion, cut crosswise into 1-inch-thick slices

½ cup lightly salted or unsalted dry-roasted peanuts

¼ cup benne (sesame) seeds

½ bunch fresh flat-leaf parsley, roughly chopped

½ bunch fresh cilantro, roughly chopped

Grated zest and juice of 1 lemon

¼ cup extra-virgin olive oil

Kosher salt

—

4 wreckfish fillets, 6–8 oz each

Avocado oil, for the grill, fish, and vegetables

Kosher salt and freshly ground black pepper

Fresh celery leaves, for garnish

Meanwhile, grill the fish. Place the wreckfish on the grate and cook, turning once, until golden brown on both sides, 4–5 minutes on each side. Be cautious when flipping, as sticking sometimes occurs. We use our fish spatula (page 183) here, and before we flip, we scrape underneath the fish from all sides to ensure we've removed it from any stuck points on the grate. When the fish is done, allow it to rest for 5 minutes.

To finish the romesco, in a blender, combine the charred onion and chiles, peanuts, benne seeds, parsley, cilantro, lemon zest and juice, and olive oil and blend on high speed until smooth and creamy, about 2 minutes. Taste for salt and season to your liking.

To serve, smear romesco across the bottom of a serving plate, place the fish on top, smear a little romesco on top of the fish, and season generously with the dukkah. Garnish with celery leaves and serve family-style.

TILEFISH WITH PECAN SALSA MACHA

Tilefish is one of our all-time-favorite Southern species. Its meat is pleasantly mild and sweet, with a firm but tender texture, and is often noted as being similar in flavor to lobster or crab. Given that tilefish is primarily sold fresh, and usually whole, you may not be familiar with it. However, it can be found at specialty seafood markets and at some of our trusted online retailers (page 15). Most often caught using longline gear, tilefish are harvested year-round throughout the Gulf, from the west coast of Florida to Campeche, Mexico. Here, our creative inspiration comes from the Gulf of Mexico, where our cravings for coastal cuisine take us to the Mexican state of Veracruz.

Although salsa macha is well established in the states of Oaxaca and Michoacán, it is commonly thought to have originated in Veracruz. It consists of a variety of dried chiles, seeds, nuts, garlic, and seasonings, all of which are finely chopped and bound together with oil. From the Spanish verb *machacar*, which means "to crush," salsa macha is traditionally stone-ground by hand using a mortar and pestle. Delicious and versatile, it's often enjoyed with seafood, tacos, quesadillas, roasted meats, and even soup. Here, we slather it on tilefish as it grills over an open hardwood fire. This technique allows for the rich oils of the salsa to baste the fish. Our version includes pecans and benne seeds for Southern terroir.

We love to make this dish the centerpiece of a family-style meal. We surround it with lime wedges, cilantro, green onions, and chiles in small bowls, a big dish of steamed Carolina Gold rice, and a stack of freshly warmed heirloom corn tortillas, and then invite guests to make their own tacos. Don't forget the hot sauce!

To make the salsa, in a food processor, combine the pecans, benne seeds, crushed and ground chiles, kosher salt, and garlic and process until finely chopped, 15–20 seconds. Add the oil and vinegar and process until well blended, about 20 seconds more. The salsa can be made in advance and stored in an airtight container in a cool, dark cupboard for up to 3 months.

Prepare a fire in your fire kettle or charcoal grill according to our Hardwood Grilling instructions on page 193. Once the heat source is roaring and your grill surface registers between 400° and 500°F, lightly brush or mist the grill grate with oil.

Makes 2–4 servings

FOR THE SALSA MACHA

1 cup pecans

2 tablespoons benne (sesame) seeds

6 fresh or dried cascabel chiles, stemmed (optional)

½ cup crushed guajillo chile (4–6 whole chile)

1 tablespoon crushed ancho chile (about 1 whole chile)

1 teaspoon ground chipotle chile

¾ teaspoon kosher salt

¾ teaspoon granulated garlic

1 cup avocado oil, plus more for the grill and fish

1 tablespoon apple cider vinegar

―

1 skin-on whole side tilefish, 1½–2¼ lb, or 4–6 skin-on tilefish fillets, 6–8 oz each

Kosher salt and freshly ground black pepper

Fresh lime juice, for dousing the fish, plus 1 lime, cut into wedges, for serving

½ cup roughly chopped fresh cilantro

Lightly rub the fish on both sides with oil and then lightly season both sides with salt and pepper. Place the fish on the grate and cook until golden brown on the first side, 6–8 minutes if cooking a whole side or 4–5 minutes if cooking fillets. Now flip the fish, working cautiously as sticking sometimes occurs. We use our fish spatula (page 183) here, and before we flip, we scrape underneath the fish from all sides to ensure we've removed it from any stuck points on the grate.

Once the fish is flipped, splash it with lime juice and then generously spoon the salsa across the entire top side (you will not need all of it). Cook the fish until golden brown on the second side, 6–8 minutes if a whole side and 4–5 minutes if fillets.

While the fish finishes cooking, put the cilantro, sliced chile, green onions, and lime wedges in separate small bowls and set them on the table. When the fish is ready, transfer it to a serving platter, sprinkle the top with the benne seeds, sea salt, and pepper, and serve.

1 Fresno or jalapeño chile, thinly sliced

2 green onions, white and green parts, thinly sliced

1 tablespoon benne (sesame) seeds

Flaky sea salt

BACKYARD CHARLESTON OYSTER ROAST

Gather around the shucking table y'all because there's nothing quite like a backyard oyster roast, Charleston-style. It's a time to come together with family and friends to share in the joy of great company and wonderful food. Imagine the sound of shells clinking together, the laughter of loved ones, and the sizzle of oysters roasting on the fire. And thanks to our friends over at Charleston Oyster Tables, we're well-equipped with a head-turning table for our friends to belly up to, making our backyard oyster roasts truly unforgettable. There's nothing on the market like what this company makes: the tables are luxurious, customizable in every sense of the word, and make a beautiful centerpiece around which to bring together friends and family.

No backyard oyster roast is complete without plenty of accoutrements and beverages. People vary on what they like with their oysters, so have plenty of hot sauce, lemon wedges, cocktail sauce, and mignonette on hand. And while some folks like to follow their oyster roast with a pig pickin', we prefer to stick with the seafood route, opting for a seafood boil (pages 138–140), gumbo (page 130), or perloo (page 133).

Prepare a fire in your fire kettle or charcoal grill according to our Hardwood Grilling instructions on page 193. Oysters can be roasted on a grill grate or griddle, so use whichever you have or prefer.

Once the heat source is roaring and the grill surface registers between 400° and 500°F, dump the oysters across the grate, spreading them out with long grill tongs to achieve a single, even layer. If cooking on an open-air fire kettle or pit, place a burlap sack soaked in water on top of the oysters. This will provide a bit of slowly disbursed steam throughout the cooking process, which helps the oysters cook evenly. If cooking on a grill with a lid, close the lid but be sure to keep the lid vent fully open so as not to suffocate the fire.

There are many contributing factors to consider when roasting oysters this way. First, keep in mind both the size of the oysters and your desired doneness. We typically roast wild-harvested clusters or large-cup farm-raised, and we prefer to cook them to a doneness of medium. That is, they are warmed through and have the consistency of a cooked oyster on the outside yet are

Recipe continues

24–48 oysters per person, wild harvested or farm raised

FOR SERVING

Variety of hot sauces, homemade (pages 245–247) and/or store-bought

Chunky Creole Cocktail Sauce (page 244)

Mignonette (page 245)

Saltine crackers, straight from the box or Cajun fried (page 176)

still plump and juicy on the inside. When cooking oysters to medium, the shells won't necessarily open, so you can't use that as a visual indicator of their doneness. Instead, we find that oysters roasted in a single layer will cook to medium in 10–12 minutes and to well done in 18–22 minutes. If you are unsure of their doneness, remove an oyster and shuck it to determine if it's cooked to medium. If cooking to well done, you'll know they are ready when the shells have opened.

Oysters can also be roasted on a pellet grill, gas grill, or gas griddle. If roasting on a pellet grill, set the temperature to 400°F and cook with the lid closed until the desired doneness is reached. We find that oysters reach medium doneness in a pellet grill in 5–7 minutes and well done in 10–12 minutes. If roasting on a gas grill or griddle, turn all burners on high and allow to heat for 5 minutes. If grilling, close the lid once the oysters have been arranged on the grate. If griddling, you can either layer a wet burlap sack on top of the oysters or pour a cup or two of water over them to provide steam as they cook. They will be ready in about the same time as when using a charcoal grill.

Pile the oysters on a big platter and surround them with a variety of sauces and plain or fried saltines and enjoy.

SEA ISLAND FORGE

Sea Island Forge, a venture fueled by passion, ingenuity, and a love for outdoor cooking, was founded by the dynamic duo Steve and Sandy Schoettle. Renowned for his expert metalwork and artistic flair, Steve is a familiar name in custom metal craftsmanship, while Sandy's background in photography and art infuses the brand with a keen eye for design. Their shared affection for coastal living is the driving force behind Sea Island Forge, permeating their dedication to community and connection.

At the core of Sea Island Forge's offerings is the 30-gallon kettle, a revolutionary piece that transcends the boundaries of outdoor cooking. Modeled after a nineteenth-century sugar kettle, it is meticulously fashioned from cast ductile iron, ensuring longevity for generations. Beyond robust materials, the kettle's standout feature lies in its thoughtful design.

The kettle boasts a boot rail for safe foot placement, and a patented ratcheting grill simplifies temperature regulation. Complemented by eye-catching accessories like the oyster fire poker and sop mop, the kettle embodies Sea Island Forge's commitment to excellence and innovation.

Yet Sea Island Forge is more than just a product line; it reflects the hospitality and generosity of its founders. Steve and Sandy welcomed us into their world with a familiarity and openness that's hard to find outside of the South, providing expertise and inviting us into their St. Simons Island home for a warm dinner and fireside chat. This warmth extends to their products, making Sea Island Forge an incredibly trustworthy brand.

The Sea Island Forge kettle has transformed our outdoor space, enhancing our cooking and entertaining experiences. The team's community spirit is palpable, offering advice and fostering a connection over the kettle. As they continue to innovate, Sea Island Forge remains dedicated to quality, sustainability, and uniting people.

PELLET GRILLING & SMOKING

Over the past decade, the popularity of pellet grills has skyrocketed, and for good reason. With the touch of a button and the spin of a dial, you can grill or smoke anything, with any variety of wood imaginable, and with great precision. Pellet grills require electricity to function but rely on compressed hardwood pellets to provide heat, smoke, and flavor. If there's just one backyard cooking instrument that you absolutely must invest in, we'd say it's a high-quality pellet smoker. It's one of those things you don't realize you've been missing out on until you get one. Simply put, the versatility, consistency, and efficiency can't be beat.

When researching which pellet grill to purchase, we found plenty of great options on the market. Ultimately, we chose one from Recteq, based out of Georgia. The quality and diversity in Recteq's product offerings are just as impressive as those of other industry leaders, such as Traeger and Weber. But its blue-ribbon warranty and customer service are unbeatable. When it comes to a pellet grill, there's much that can go wrong, from the hopper getting jammed up and not churning properly to the thermocouple going kaput to an electric component burning out, so these two company qualities are critical.

When we make an investment in such an expensive, constantly used piece of equipment, it's important that we feel like more than just another online transaction. At Recteq, it truly seems like anyone passionate about cooking can develop a rapport with the in-house team. They exude the same sense of Southern hospitality that we provide at our restaurants, and if you encounter a problem, they're committed to making it right. Recteq also likes to say that once you join the family, you're a member for life. To us, there's just something invaluable about the human experience, and we can confidently tell you that if you're cut from that same cloth, you'll find what you're looking for with the folks at Recteq.

Capable of everything from high-heat grilling to low-and-slow barbecue pit–style smoking, a pellet grill will keep you from getting bored with cooking. You'll find a ton of recipes and tips out there at your disposal, and given it's often as simple as following directions, we're only showcasing a few recipes here. With that being said, you could cook delicious seafood on your pellet grill three days a week year-round and most likely never hit a wall.

SWEET & SPICY FISH COLLARS

If you're on the hunt for a new, delicious cut of fish, look no further than the humble fish collar. Although it was once discarded as scrap, this underrated cut has rightfully gained some serious popularity in recent years. As the name suggests, fish collars are taken from along the clavicle of fish. They're a bit new to the market, so you may have to do some digging to get your hands on them. Check your local specialty seafood markets, or take matters into your own hands and remove the collars from whole fish yourself. To get the most out of the collar, you'll want to remove the gills and fillets first, then carefully slice away the meat, fin, and bone around the head. Pro tip: leave a bit of extra meat near the head to yield a larger, more succulent collar cut.

Fish collars offer a wide range of flavors and textures, from tender and mild to rich and fatty, thanks to the belly meat found at the tip of the cut. And unlike other cuts, collars don't contain small bones, making them easier to enjoy on the bone. Eating collars is a messy and fun affair, similar to getting down and dirty with some ribs or wings. Our go-to collars come from snapper, bass, cobia, amberjack, and salmon.

Preheat your pellet grill to 300°F. This recipe can also be cooked on a standard charcoal or gas grill. Just be mindful of your heat source and expect the fish to cook faster.

While the grill is heating, in a bowl, combine the honey, lime zest and juice, cilantro, garlic, chile, and salt and mix well. This is your sauce. We often refer to it as a honey-chile-lime glaze. It's also phenomenal on wings.

Lay the fish collars on a sheet pan and generously season both sides with the sauce.

When the grill is ready, place the collars, flesh side down, on the rack, close the lid, and cook for 10 minutes. Open the lid, carefully flip the collars, close the lid, and cook for another 10 minutes.

Transfer the collars to a large serving plate. Generously coat the flesh side of each collar with the sauce and serve immediately.

Makes 2–4 servings

½ cup honey

Grated zest and juice of 1 lime

½ cup finely chopped fresh cilantro

2 cloves garlic, finely grated

1 Fresno chile, minced

½ teaspoon kosher salt

6–12 fish collars, 4–8 oz each

Coconut Rib Rub, for coating the collars (page 241)

SMOKED BLUEHOUSE SALMON BRAVAS

Fishing for wild sea-run Atlantic salmon has been prohibited in the United States since 1948. Known as the King of Fish, this magnificent species has faced great decline in the wild, and in the United States, native Atlantic salmon populations are limited to a few rivers in Maine. Because of this, they are listed as endangered under the Endangered Species Act, and the only Atlantic salmon available on the market today are farm raised.

Enter Bluehouse Salmon, an innovative land-based Atlantic salmon farm located in Homestead, Florida. Its salmon are raised in a recirculating aquaculture system (RAS) that uses advanced technology to filter and recirculate water, providing a clean, controlled, and eco-friendly environment for the fish to grow without the need for antibiotics. The fish are healthy, rich, and delicious and can be enjoyed in a variety of preparations, from sashimi style to hardwood smoked. Bluehouse products are widely available at grocery stores throughout the continental United States and can be located through the company's online tracker. We love getting our hands on the whole salmon and butchering them ourselves. The bones are perfect for our White Wine Fish Stock (page 135), the extra-fatty neck and cheeks are ideal for our Sweet & Spicy Fish Collars (page 209), the belly is fabulous for making salmon bacon, the center-cut loin is insanely delicious for crudo, and, of course, we love smoking a whole side in our pellet grill. As with many of our Mediterranean-inspired fish preparations, we often accompany this dish with a simple salad and roasted or fried potatoes.

Set a wire rack on a large sheet pan. Pat both sides of the salmon dry with paper towels and place the fish on the rack. Refrigerate uncovered overnight.

When you are ready to begin smoking the next day, preheat your pellet grill (or smoker) to 225°F. Meanwhile, make the brine. In a small saucepan, combine the water, sugar, and salt and bring to a simmer over medium heat, whisking until the sugar and salt dissolve. Pour in the honey while whisking constantly. Remove the pan from the heat and set it near the pellet grill along with a basting brush.

Recipe continues

Makes 4–6 servings

1 whole side salmon (preferably from Bluehouse), 2–3 lb

Avocado oil, for the fish

½ cup fresh basil leaves

½ cup fresh flat-leaf parsley leaves

2 green onions, white and green parts, thinly sliced

1 tablespoon extra-virgin olive oil

Grated zest and juice of 1 lemon

Kosher salt and freshly ground black pepper

FOR THE SMOKING BRINE

1 cup water

½ cup sugar

½ cup kosher salt

¼ cup honey

Lightly coat the skin side of the fish with avocado oil, rubbing it into the skin to create an even coat. This helps prevent the fish from sticking to the rack while cooking. Place the fish, skin side down, on the top rack of the grill and generously baste with the brine. Close the lid and set a timer for 15 minutes. Once the timer goes off, generously baste the fish with the brine. Repeat this step, basting every 15 minutes for the first hour of cooking, for a total of five bastes. After 1 hour, baste with the brine every 30 minutes until the salmon is done. We like to smoke whole sides of salmon for a minimum of 2 hours and to an internal temperature of 145ºF.

While the salmon smokes, prepare the sauce. In a food processor, combine the crushed tomatoes, tomato paste, red peppers, olive oil, garlic, sugar, vinegar, and paprika and process until a smooth and shiny sauce forms. Taste and season with salt to your liking. We prefer this sauce served at room temperature, but it can also be served chilled or heated. It can be made up to 2 weeks in advance and stored in an airtight container in the refrigerator.

When the fish is ready, transfer it to a wire rack set on a sheet pan and let rest for 15 minutes before serving.

To serve, in a bowl, combine the basil, parsley, green onions, olive oil, and lemon zest and juice. Gently toss together and lightly season with salt and black pepper. Spoon a generous amount of the sauce across the bottom of a serving platter and place the side of salmon on top. Scatter the herb mixture across the salmon and serve immediately.

FOR THE SAUCE

1 cup canned crushed tomatoes (see Note)

2 tablespoons tomato paste

½ cup fire-roasted red peppers

½ cup extra-virgin olive oil

1 clove garlic

1 tablespoon sugar

1 teaspoon sherry vinegar

1 teaspoon smoked paprika (preferably pimentón de la Vera)

Kosher salt

Note: Bianco DiNapoli canned tomatoes are our pantry's hidden gem, elevating everything from rice dishes and stews to casseroles and sauces. Grown organically in the sun-drenched soils of Northern California, the tomatoes' unparalleled richness is born from the perfect blend of long summer days and fertile earth. Beyond their sustainable production, we cherish these tomatoes for their irresistibly lush flavor and luxurious mouthfeel. Infused with sweet and juicy notes, they promise to enhance the succulence of every dish that embraces the magic of canned tomatoes.

SMOKING FISH

Our fish-smoking technique is universal to any cut of fish, from a fillet to a whole side. We've found that most cuts cook to an acceptable doneness—an internal temperature of 145°F—at a rate of about one hour per pound. Smoking fish at 225°F ensures the heat is delicate enough not to dry out the fish, and we prefer smoking our fish for a minimum of two hours, which is what it takes to develop the rich, smoky flavor we're after. For this reason, we tend to avoid smoking pieces of fish any smaller than one pound unless they are whole dressed fish, such as trout. As with most cuts of meat, when the bones are still intact, more insulation is provided around the meat, which often translates to better moisture retention. As always, we urge you to cook with intuition and intention.

To start the process, set a wire rack on a sheet pan. Pat your fish dry with paper towels and place it on the rack. Refrigerate uncovered overnight to form what is referred to as a pellicle, a tacky coating of proteins on the surface of fish that helps smoke stick while also contributing to a rich color and flavor.

The next day, preheat the pellet grill (or smoker) to 225°F. Place a small amount of neutral high-heat cooking oil (such as avocado oil) on the skin side of the fish and rub to coat the skin evenly. This will prevent sticking. Place the fish, skin side down, on the top rack of the grill. Close the lid and set a timer for 15 minutes. Once the timer goes off, generously baste the fish with brine. Repeat this step, basting every 15 minutes, for the first hour of cooking, for a total of four bastes. After 1 hour, baste every 30 minutes. When basting fish, be sure to brush away any white, foamy scuzz that forms on the top of the fish. This is a protein called albumin that coagulates and rises to the surface during cooking. From a presentation perspective, it's not very appealing to the eye. Our method of repeated basting with brine removes this substance and produces a gorgeous, glossy golden brown lacquer.

When your fish is smoked to your liking, once again set it on a wire rack atop a sheet pan and let it rest for 15 minutes before serving. Because of the salt content in our brine, our smoked fish will keep in the refrigerator for up to a week. We enjoy freshly smoked fish while still warm, but we often cook enough for chilled fish preparations too. Toss some into your scrambled eggs or smear it on a bagel for breakfast, scatter it over your salad for lunch, or even make a Dagwood-style smoked fish BLT. However you decide to enjoy your smoked fish, we think you'll agree that it makes meal prep quick, easy, and delicious.

COCONUT UNAGI BARBECUED POMPANO

The Florida pompano is a member of the jack family, and although it is most commonly harvested along the coast of Florida, its migratory patterns span from Massachusetts to Brazil. Pompano meat is firm and somewhat sweet, with a finely flaked texture, and we find that it's an excellent choice for whole preparations. The most common catch size hovers right around two pounds, the high fat content allows for cooking it well done without drying out, and the meat peels right off the bone.

Here, we develop a tacky glaze inspired by the flavor profiles of a Japanese unagi roll while relying on the low-and-slow techniques of a Southern barbecue pit to smoke the fish to perfection. By calling for coconut sugar and coconut aminos, our unagi sauce boasts luscious Caribbean vibes. The sweet and smoky notes are elevated to perfection with charred lime, benne seeds, and green onions. We often serve this recipe with steamed Carolina Gold rice and just-ripe avocado—a healthy, delicious meal that's simple enough to prepare any night of the week.

Slip the fish into a gallon-size resealable plastic bag. To make the marinade, in a bowl, whisk together the ale, brown sugar, oil, and salt until well mixed and the sugar has dissolved. Pour the marinade into the bag with the fish, press out the air, seal the bag, and marinate in the refrigerator overnight.

Meanwhile, make the sauce. In a blender, combine the coconut sugar, coconut aminos, and miso and blend on high speed until the sugar dissolves and all the ingredients are well blended, about 1½ minutes. Transfer to an airtight container and refrigerate until needed. It will keep for up to 3 months.

When you are ready to cook the fish the next day, preheat your pellet grill to 300°F. This recipe can also be cooked on a standard charcoal or gas grill. Just be mindful of your heat source and expect the fish to cook faster.

Remove the fish from its marinade and lay it on the grill. Close the lid and cook for 10 minutes. Open the lid, baste with some of the sauce, flip the fish, baste with more of the sauce, and close the lid. Repeat this step three more times, basting, flipping, basting, and cooking in 10-minute increments, for a total cooking time of 40 minutes. From here, test the temperature of your fish. If the thermometer registers 145°F or higher, it's ready to pull. If not, continue this

Makes 2–4 servings

1 whole pompano, 2–2½ lb, dressed

FOR THE MARINADE

1½–2 cups dark ale

½ cup firmly packed dark brown sugar

2 tablespoons avocado oil

1 teaspoon kosher salt

FOR THE SAUCE

1 cup coconut sugar

½ cup coconut aminos

2 tablespoons red miso

FOR GARNISH

1 lime

Kosher salt, freshly ground black pepper, and avocado oil, for the lime

2 tablespoons benne (sesame) seeds

2 green onions, white and green parts, thinly sliced

process, checking the temperature every 10 minutes with each baste and flip. Depending on the size of the fish and the precision of your tools, this process can take 40–60 minutes.

To smoke the lime for garnish, cut it in half and lightly season the cut sides with salt, pepper, and oil. Add the lime to the grill, cut side down, after the fish has cooked for 10 minutes, and smoke the lime for 30 minutes.

To serve, transfer the fish to a serving platter and let rest for 5 minutes. Then drizzle with a few more tablespoons of the sauce. Garnish with the benne seeds and green onions, scattering them across the fish, and accompany with the smoked lime for squeezing.

BENNE SEEDS

Benne seeds are an heirloom ancestor of sesame that grew wild throughout sub-Saharan Africa. The word *benne* means "sesame" in Bantu, a West African language, and is traditionally associated with good fortune. Enslaved Africans brought benne seeds to the West Indies and the southern United States in the late seventeenth century and grew them in their gardens. By the late eighteenth century, benne seeds and their oil had become staples in Lowcountry food and a focus of intense market farming. In the nineteenth century, benne oil was the go-to salad dressing of the South, but the production of cottonseed oil eventually overtook the market.

Heirloom African benne seeds carry lovely field flavors and collect characteristic nuttiness and burnt-honey notes when toasted. When it comes to suitability for use in recipes modern and archival, Anson Mills benne seeds are unmatched. We frequently reach for them in our kitchen when cooking classic Southern, Mediterranean, Asian, and even Mexican meals.

WOOD-FIRED OVEN COOKERY

We've long dreamed of wood-fired oven cooking in our backyard, and thanks to the fine folks over at Fontana Forni, we're living that dream.

In 1978, in the small town of San Lorenzo in Campo, Italy, the Fontana brothers designed and built the first-ever indirect combustion oven, and since then, this family-owned operation has continued to innovate and raise the bar for Italian-built wood-fired ovens. Funny enough, we discovered them because of their Florence outpost—Florence, South Carolina, that is.

Located just a few hours from where we call home, the team over at Fontana Forni's US headquarters have been world-class to work with. They held our hands throughout selecting the perfect oven for us, and have continued to provide us with expert guidance as we hit our learning curve. Their ovens are all made in Italy and feature, hands down, the best construction, design, and materials we've seen. The company also offers a wide variety of options, so you'll find exactly what you're looking for.

It's been a dream come true to stoke up our Fontana Forni and come back to center through simple, rustic hardwood roasting and baking. Obviously, the pizzas are insane, but we love the flavor that hardwood roasting imparts to everything from seafood, meat, and poultry to vegetables. It comes as no surprise that we have found no cookware is better-suited to our oven than cast iron. If a wood-fired oven has been your dream, too, we encourage you to look no further than Fontana Forni.

TOPNECK CLAMS AL FORNO

In northern Italy, along the Adriatic coast of Veneto, there's a culinary tradition that celebrates the simple pleasures of *frutti di mare*, literally "fruits of the sea." This phrase often refers to bivalves, and when it comes to Italian shellfish preparations, we think clams are king. This dish brings together Italian sausage, plump topneck clams, and a host of aromatic vegetables in a savory white-wine cream sauce. Roasted to perfection in a cast-iron skillet, this rustic Italian riff relies on a healthy dose of both the holy trinity and hardwood hickory to deliver the bold flavors of the Southern kitchen.

Preheat your wood-fired oven to 400°F. This preparation can also be cooked in a standard home kitchen oven.

In a 12- to 14-inch cast-iron skillet or sauté pan, pour in enough of the oil to coat the bottom. Place the pan in the oven and heat for 5 minutes. Remove the pan from the oven and add the sausages to it. Return the pan to the oven and sear the sausages on the first side until golden brown, 3–5 minutes. Remove from the oven, flip the sausages, and add the onion, celery, chile, and garlic (cut side down). Return the pan to the oven and sweat the onion, celery, and chile until translucent and sear the second side of the sausages until golden brown, 3–5 minutes.

Remove the pan from the oven, pour in the wine, and deglaze the pan, scraping up any browned bits (fond) from the pan bottom. Place the bundle of thyme in the center of the pan. Return the pan to the oven and allow the wine to reduce by half. Remove from the oven, add the clams and cream, and then return the pan to the oven until the sauce is simmering and the clams have opened, 12–15 minutes. Remove from the oven and discard any clams that failed to open. Season to taste with salt and pepper.

Enjoy this dish family-style, placing the pan on a trivet in the center of the table. Serve with plenty of bread for dipping and an empty bowl for the discarded shells.

Makes 2–4 servings

2–3 tablespoons avocado oil

1 lb sweet or spicy Italian sausages

½ Vidalia or other sweet onion, diced

2 celery ribs, diced

1 Anaheim chile, diced

1 head garlic, cut through the equator to expose all the cloves

1 cup dry white wine

½ bunch fresh thyme, tied together with kitchen string

16–24 topneck clams

½ cup heavy cream

Kosher salt and freshly ground black pepper

Crusty bread, for serving

ALL CLAMS ON DECK

Harmful algal blooms are caused by several species of algae—from blue-green to red—and have been a thorn in the side of marine conservationists for decades. These toxic blooms, which can sometimes turn marine waters into a crimson soup (red tide), wreak havoc on marine life, leaving fish, manatees, dolphins, sea turtles, and birds gasping for breath. While red tides are a natural occurrence, modern society is responsible for the increase in both their severity and frequency. Nitrogen runoff from such human sources as Big Ag, factories, and sewage treatment plants enters our waters on land and eventually flows into the ocean. This overabundance of nutrients, paired with warm water, fuels these toxic tides by causing algae to multiply rapidly. Florida's Gulf Coast has seen a sharp rise in red-tide incidents in recent years, but there's a ray of hope shining through those red waters.

Enter All Clams on Deck, a nonprofit organization that's doing its darnedest to restore the health of the Gulf of Mexico. By promoting coastal resiliency, restoring bivalve habitats, and educating the public about the importance of seagrass meadows, All Clams on Deck is making waves in the conservation world. Their goal? To create a future where shellfish and seagrass are abundant, ecosystems are healthy, and coastal communities thrive.

All Clams on Deck is focused on creating healthier estuaries that in turn can help reduce harmful algae blooms. Like all bivalves, clams are filter feeders, and according to our good friend and founding member Ed Chiles, they can be used as a biological mitigation strategy to achieve cleaner waters. As more clams are planted and waters become cleaner, more sunlight can make its way through the water column, allowing for seagrass to flourish.

Seagrass meadows are a vital part of the ocean's ecosystem, serving as its "lungs" by pumping out oxygen and sequestering carbon at a rate that puts the Amazonian rainforest to shame (that is, over thirty-five times faster). Seagrass meadows are also essential in helping to reduce flooding, providing nursery habitats for fish, improving water quality, and supporting over one million species.

The folks over at All Clams on Deck make a strong, science-based case that clams and seagrass have the potential to bolster the Tampa Bay, Sarasota Bay, Charlotte Harbor, and Indian River Lagoon national estuaries. They're calling on citizens and policymakers at the national, state, and local level to help them plant more clams—a lot more clams—and that's a call we should all heed. Florida's coastlines boast a million acres of aquaculture-approved waters, but only 1 percent of that space is currently leased. With an unwavering commitment to sustainable aquaculture practices, this collective of community activists is taking the lead in solving Florida's red-tide climate crisis, one clam at a time.

SALT-CRUSTED BLACK SEA BASS ESCABECHE

Black sea bass is known for its delicate flavor and tender, succulent meat. In the United States, it's fished sustainably from Massachusetts to the Gulf Coast of Florida using responsible catch methods, including rod and reel, longline, and handline. If you can't get your hands on a black sea bass, striped sea bass, snapper, or rockfish is an excellent substitute.

Salt-baking whole fish as we do here is inspired by a technique developed by Spanish fishermen, with origins and influences dating back to the ancient Roman salt flats of the Murcia region on Spain's Mediterranean coast. In this recipe, we encase a whole black sea bass in a smoky, garlicky salt mixture, which, in the heat of the oven, forms a hard crust that simultaneously steams the fish and infuses it with a deep, rich seasoning. The result is a melt-in-your-mouth whole fish that pairs perfectly with our lemony, honeyed escabeche sauce.

Escabeche, which stems from Spanish and Portuguese kitchens, traditionally calls for frying fish or meat, marinating it in a sweetened acidic sauce, and then serving it cold. This beloved sweet-and-sour smack has been adopted and adapted by cooks throughout Latin America, the Philippines, and beyond. Nowadays, escabeche is prepared with fish, meat, or vegetables, which can be marinated, pickled, cooked in, or smothered in a tart yet sweet sauce. In Mexico, escabeche refers to a medley of spicy pickled vegetables that are heaped atop everything from roasted pork to fish tacos.

Here, we smother our cooked whole fish in a sweet and tangy sauce that includes raw peppers and onions, a technique most commonly found in Jamaica and the Philippines. Easy to prepare and striking to present, this dish will impress guests at a dinner party. Serve it family-style accompanied with lightly dressed lettuces and roasted potatoes.

Preheat your wood-fired oven to 400°F. This preparation can also be cooked in a standard home kitchen oven.

Recipe continues

Makes 2–4 servings

4 cups kosher salt

1 tablespoon granulated garlic

1 tablespoon smoked paprika

1 cup water

1 black sea bass, 2–2½ lb, dressed

FOR THE ESCABECHE

1 red bell pepper, julienned

½ red onion, julienned

1 Fresno chile, julienned

1 Scotch bonnet or habanero chile, minced (optional)

½ cup finely chopped fresh flat-leaf parsley

2 cloves garlic, finely grated with a zester

Grated zest and juice of 1 lemon

¼ cup honey

¼ cup extra-virgin olive oil

1 teaspoon kosher salt

In a bowl, combine the salt, granulated garlic, paprika, and water and mix together until all the ingredients are fully incorporated and the mixture is the consistency of wet sand. Place about 1 cup of the salt mixture on the base of a cast-iron sizzler, a casserole, or a sheet pan. Use whatever you have on hand and prefer, making sure it is larger than your fish so it can accommodate the salt crust. Press the base layer of salt into the shape and size of your whole fish, then place the fish on top. Pour the remaining salt mixture onto the fish and press around to form an even top coat. Place in the oven and roast for 30 minutes.

Meanwhile, prepare the escabeche. In a bowl, combine all the ingredients and toss together until well mixed. Allow to marinate at room temperature while the fish cooks.

Remove the fish from the oven and let rest for 10 minutes. Then, using the back of a large spoon, tap the salt crust to crack it open and remove it completely from the top and sides of the fish. Top the fish with the escabeche and its juices and serve family-style directly from the cooking vessel.

OYSTER BED BIENVILLE WITH TEXAS TOAST

Our love for New Orleans cuisine runs deep, and when we discovered the oyster bed at the restaurant Saffron NOLA, it only intensified that passion. This innovative cooking device cradles your oysters perfectly, ensuring they cook evenly and stay juicy. And what better way to showcase these beauties than with our riff on the classic oysters Bienville? We start by bathing shucked oysters in a creamy lobster bisque sauce spiked with Worcestershire, parsley, green onions, and pinches of salt and pepper. The oysters are then nestled in the pockets of the oyster bed and generously coated in a blanket of Parmigiano-Reggiano. Roasted until golden brown and crispy, these luxurious oysters are a taste of the Gulf Coast good life. To round out the experience, we serve the oysters with slices of garlicky Texas toast—perfect for soaking up all that saucy, savory goodness.

Preheat your wood-fired oven to 400°F. This preparation can also be cooked in a standard home kitchen oven.

In a saucepan over medium heat, bring the lobster bisque to a gentle simmer. Add the butter, Worcestershire sauce, parsley, and green onions and stir until the butter melts. Add the oysters, salt, and pepper, return to a simmer, and remove from the heat. Spoon the oysters into the pockets of an oyster bed. Or pour the contents of the pan into an 8- to 10-inch cast-iron skillet. Sprinkle the cheese across the top of everything saucy.

Place the oysters in the oven and roast until the bisque is hot and bubbly and the cheese is golden brown, 12–15 minutes.

While the oysters are roasting, make the toast. In a small saucepan over medium heat, melt the butter with the garlic. When the butter is melted, remove from the heat. Baste both sides of each bread slice with the garlic butter and season with salt and pepper. Lay the slices on a sheet pan.

Place the sheet pan in the oven and bake the toast, flipping each slice about halfway through cooking, until golden brown and crispy on both sides, about 7 minutes. Remove from the oven and cut each slice in half.

Serve the oysters family-style, landing the pan on a trivet at the center of the table. Accompany with the toast.

Makes 2–4 servings

1 can (10½ oz) Bar Harbor semi-condensed lobster bisque

2 tablespoons salted butter

Dash of Worcestershire sauce

¼ cup finely chopped fresh flat-leaf parsley

2 green onions, white and green parts, thinly sliced

1 pack or jar (8 oz) freshly shucked oysters, drained and rinsed

Pinch of kosher salt

Pinch of freshly ground black pepper

2 cups grated Parmigiano-Reggiano cheese

FOR THE TEXAS TOAST

6 tablespoons salted butter

4 cloves garlic, finely grated with a zester

4–6 slices crusty white bread (preferably freshly cut from a whole loaf), each 1½ inches thick

Kosher salt and freshly ground black pepper

SUNDRIES

LIKE THE REVERED MOM-AND-POP PROVISIONS shops you find on most Main Streets in small Southern towns, consider the pages of Sundries to be a place you'll frequent often, and even sometimes unexpectedly. Recipes in other chapters will send you here for a needed component, but you'll also flip through these pages to get your fix of fixins, step up your seasoning game, and even trick out your refrigerator door. We like to think of our Sundries recipes as a hodgepodge of our favorite Southern staples—the stuff that legendary potlucks are made of.

While feasting on seafood, folks often require a great variety of sides and accoutrements. Sundries allows eaters to fill out their dinner tables or plates and create what seems like an infinite amount of flavor combinations while in pursuit of their favorite dip, dunk, or dash.

Most likely, the pages in this chapter will become well weathered with smudged fingerprints of Lowcountry seasoning and splashes of corn bread batter, and for good reason: hot sauces, an array of sides, spice blends, and even two styles of slaw await.

EXTRA-FANCY CANDIED YAMS

With their elegant simplicity and succulent texture, these yams are a true melt-in-your-mouth Southern delicacy. While we certainly appreciate a good old-fashioned yam casserole with marshmallows and pecans, there's a time and a place for such indulgence. These yams are the ideal side to a coastal-inspired Sunday supper.

In a large saucepan, combine the yams with water to cover and lightly season the water with kosher salt. Bring to a simmer over medium heat, reduce the heat to maintain a gentle simmer, and cook the yams low and slow until tender and creamy, 20–25 minutes. To check for doneness, pierce them with a cake tester or paring knife. Using a slotted spoon or spider, transfer the yams to a sheet pan, arranging them in a single layer. Cooking the yams this way breaks down their complex carbohydrates and converts them to simple sugars, which brings out their natural sweetness and creaminess.

In a large cast-iron skillet over medium heat, melt the butter with the vanilla bean pod and scraped seeds. Place the yam medallions in the skillet and cook, constantly basting them with the vanilla brown butter and turning them once at the halfway point, until golden brown on both sides, 3–4 minutes on each side. Adjust the heat if needed to brown but not burn the butter. If the butter threatens to burn, add more cold butter to stall the process.

Using a slotted spatula, transfer the yams to a serving bowl or platter with high sides. Baste the slices one last time with the vanilla brown butter. Finish the dish by drizzling the sweet potato nectar evenly over the yams, then sprinkling with smoked sea salt, pepper, and lavender (if using). Serve right away.

Makes 2–4 servings

2 large Garnet yams, peeled and cut into 2-inch-thick medallions

Kosher salt

½ cup (4 oz) salted butter, plus more if needed

1 vanilla bean, split lengthwise and seeds scraped

¼ cup sweet potato nectar, sorghum molasses, date molasses, honey, or pure maple syrup

Smoked sea salt and freshly ground black pepper

1 teaspoon fresh or dried culinary lavender buds (optional)

LOWCOUNTRY CAST-IRON CORN BREAD

There's nothing more Lowcountry than starting your corn bread off in a hot skillet sizzling with butter. It creates a rich and crispy toffee-like crust that's possible only with cast iron. It's important to note that this isn't one of those dry-your-mouth-out-crumbly corn breads. In fact, it's the polar opposite. We developed this recipe with yellow-birthday-cake amounts of butter, eggs, and sugar in mind, so although it's already pure decadence, you can absolutely treat yourself and enjoy it with butter and honey, or even with a scoop of vanilla ice cream and some fresh-picked lavender.

Preheat the oven to 400°F.

In a liquid measuring cup, combine the melted butter and oil. In a medium bowl, whisk together the eggs and buttermilk until smooth. In a large bowl, whisk together the cornmeal, flour, sugar, baking powder, and salt. Add the buttermilk-egg mixture to the cornmeal mixture and whisk together. Stream in the butter-oil mixture while whisking constantly until smooth.

Preheat a 10- to 12-inch cast-iron skillet over medium heat for 2 minutes. Add the 1 tablespoon butter. When the butter has melted, pour in the corn bread batter and let cook for 1 minute. This creates an amazing crust!

Transfer the skillet to the oven and bake the corn bread until a toothpick inserted into the center comes out clean, 25–30 minutes. But the timing can vary depending on the size of the skillet and your oven. The corn bread can cook as fast as 20 minutes and as slow as 40 minutes, so use your gut and cook with intuition.

Place the skillet on a trivet and allow the corn bread to rest and relax at room temperature for 30 minutes before cutting.

Makes 6–8 servings

½ cup (4 oz) salted butter, melted, plus 1 tablespoon for the skillet

¼ cup avocado or canola oil

2 large eggs

2 cups buttermilk

1 cup fine-grind heirloom yellow cornmeal

1 cup all-purpose flour

¾ cup organic sugar

1 tablespoon baking powder

1 teaspoon kosher salt

PEPSI-COLA SEA ISLAND RED PEAS

The Sea Island Red Pea, an heirloom crop native to the Gullah corridor of the Sea Islands, is a beloved staple of the coastal Southern diet. With Pepsi having roots in the nearby coastal town of New Bern, North Carolina, it's only fitting to pair the two for an authentic taste experience. To bring out the deep, rich caramelization that the peas deserve, be sure to use Pepsi made with real sugar. The result is a dish that represents the best of both traditional Southern cuisine and modern culinary preferences. Start cooking the peas in the morning and leave them on the stove all day until evening if you don't want to keep them cooking overnight.

In a large stockpot or Dutch oven over medium heat, melt the bacon grease. Add the onion, celery, bell pepper, chile (if using), garlic, and bacon and sauté until the vegetables and bacon are light golden brown, 5–7 minutes. Add the peas, Pepsi, stock, sugar, molasses, vanilla, and bay leaf and bring to a simmer. Add 2 teaspoons salt and 1 teaspoon black pepper to start the seasoning and stir to ensure all the ingredients are well incorporated. Turn down the heat to maintain a gentle simmer, cover, and cook low and slow overnight, stirring every hour or so (except when sleeping).

In the morning, uncover the pot and continue cooking until the liquid reduces and your pot of Sea Island Red Peas is thick and a rich reddish brown. Before serving, taste for seasoning and add more salt and black pepper to your liking. Serve warm.

Makes 6–8 servings

2 tablespoons bacon grease or canola or other vegetable oil

1 yellow onion, diced

3 celery ribs, diced

1 green bell pepper, diced

1 jalapeño or serrano chile, diced (optional)

3 cloves garlic, finely chopped

4 slices bacon, diced

2 cups dried Sea Island Red Peas, picked over, then soaked overnight in water to cover, drained, and rinsed

4 cups real-sugar Pepsi-Cola

4 cups chicken stock

1 cup firmly packed light or dark brown sugar

¼ cup blackstrap molasses

1 teaspoon pure vanilla extract

1 fresh or dried bay leaf

Kosher salt and freshly ground black pepper

COCONUT GINGER COLLARDS

Far more than just a side dish, a delicious bowl of greens has the power to heal the soul. Unlike most collards recipes that call for lard, a ham hock, or a smoked turkey neck, this recipe is vibrantly vegan—not by fad but rather by foodways. Like much of the food celebrated and enjoyed throughout the South, this dish is rooted in West African ingredients and techniques that have evolved over time, generation by generation. Cooking greens with coconut milk and ginger in a more plant-forward, healthy approach is traditional to the Gullah Geechee people of the Sea Islands. We learned about this method from Charleston chef BJ Dennis, who also incorporates peanut butter in his recipe for an even richer, heartier pot of greens. Throughout our journey, we've learned that cooking greens is ceremonial—even spiritual. So be sure to cook from the heart and savor every bite.

We don't waste our collard stems. Instead, we've developed a technique that renders them tender. Start by washing your collards whole, then chop off the first 3–5 inches (depending on size) from the bottom of the bunch. This section is where the stems are thickest and most fibrous. Finely slice those stems and they'll melt. Cut the leaves into 1-inch-wide strips.

In a large stockpot or Dutch oven over medium heat, melt the coconut oil. Add the onions and sweat, stirring frequently, until translucent, about 3 minutes. Add the ginger, garlic, and chile (if using) and sweat, stirring somewhat constantly, for 1 minute. Add the collard stems and sweat, stirring somewhat constantly, for 2–3 minutes.

Add the coconut milk, collard leaves, sugar, and 1 tablespoon salt and bring to a simmer. Stir to ensure all the ingredients are well incorporated, then turn down the heat to maintain a gentle simmer, cover, and cook low and slow until the collards are tender, about 45 minutes.

Before serving, taste for seasoning and add more salt to your liking. Serve warm.

Makes 4–6 servings

2 bunches collards

¼ cup coconut oil

2 yellow onions, diced

¼ cup peeled and minced fresh ginger

¼ cup minced garlic

1 serrano chile, minced (optional)

3½ cups canned coconut milk (two 14-oz cans)

2 tablespoons coconut sugar or firmly packed light or dark brown sugar

Kosher salt

GEORGE & PINK'S

Any Edistonian will kindly let you know that you can't leave town without stopping at the local produce stand, George & Pink's, serving sundries to Edisto Island, South Carolina, for over fifty years. "Start down Highway 174, then turn right on a dirt road called Eddingsville Beach Road. Follow the hand-painted signs and stock up once you get there," says Steve Wenger, a cherished family acquaintance. Dirt roads have always served as sort of a time machine, transporting us to simpler times as soon as our tires begin to maneuver onto unpaved paths. This live oak–lined dirt road in particular, though, felt like a scene from a movie and set the tone for the experience that lay ahead.

Directly outside of the unassuming gem, a variety of pies and produce were listed on chalkboards. Upon entering, Pink stood behind the counter and greeted us with a smile we felt even behind a mask. She waited patiently and lent a helping hand while we grabbed biscuits, tomatoes, boiled peanuts, chowchow, Marsh Hen Mill grits, hot sauce, chips, and jams.

The store is named after Pink and her father, George Brown. Pink manages the store, and her brother, Bobby, farms the seven-acre plot of land from which most of the produce comes. The roots of the Brown family have been planted in Edisto for generations. Their ties to farming and the Lowcountry are inextricably linked to slavery; the maternal side of the family has been in Edisto since before the Civil War, where their forebears were enslaved at Bleak Hall Plantation.

In 2019, the family home burned down, and the community came together. The fundraising goal of $190,000 was surpassed. That's the South we celebrate.

If you're ever in the area, do yourself the favor of stopping by George & Pink's. They even accept cards at the register now. You'll be glad you stopped by.

CACIO E PEPE GRITS

Cacio e pepe is a famous Roman pasta dish prepared with heaps of grated aged hard cheese and freshly ground black pepper. It dates from ancient times and was originally the food of shepherds, who carried an iron pan and the ingredients on their long periods away from home. When applied to grits, this humble shepherds' comfort combo creates a bowl of bold and creamy soul-satisfying goodness.

Like most rice, grits usually come packaged with cooking instructions that provide the ratio of grain to liquid and the total cook time. Some grits are so coarse that they need to be soaked overnight before they will cook tender. That's why we recommend following the suggested method of the mill or farm from which they are sourced. If instructions are not on the package, they're often available online.

Once you've determined the grain-to-liquid ratio and cook time of the grits you are using, use our general method for preparing this recipe: In a large saucepan over medium heat, bring 4 cups of the milk to a gentle simmer. Slowly stream in the grits while whisking constantly. Then cook the grits for the amount of time indicated on the package instructions. Whisk the grits frequently as they cook and, if necessary, continue to add milk, ½ cup at a time, until cooked to the desired doneness.

Whisk in the butter, a few cubes at a time, and then whisk in the cheese and finally the pepper. Season with salt to your liking and serve immediately.

Makes 4 servings

4–6 cups organic whole milk

1½ cups coarse-ground heirloom grits

4 tablespoons salted butter, cut into cubes and kept cold

2 cups grated Parmigiano-Reggiano cheese

1 tablespoon freshly ground black pepper

Kosher salt

SLAW & PICKLES

We're crazy about slaws and pickles, which are non-negotiable for our epic sandwiches, fried fish plates and Sunday supper spreads alike. No store-bought stuff here—only our homemade creations make the cut. The electrifying zest and satisfying crunch in these recipes beat anything off the shelf.

Pop's Slaw

Makes 6–8 cups

With bold, zesty flavors and a distinct New Orleans flair, this slaw is a true Southern gem. Its humble beginnings can be traced back to Sammy's parents' neighborhood bar and grill, nestled alongside a True Value and a Food Lion in one of Chapel Hill's finest strip-mall plazas. Despite its unassuming origins, this slaw was the real MVP that kept the doors open for nearly a decade, a testament to its no-fuss, irresistible appeal.

½ head green cabbage, finely shredded
6 collard green leaves, stems removed and greens thinly sliced
½ red onion, thinly sliced
4 green onions, white and green parts, thinly sliced
½ jalapeño chile, minced (optional)
2 cloves garlic, finely grated with a zester
2 tablespoons peeled and finely grated fresh horseradish root, or 1 tablespoon prepared horseradish
1 cup mayonnaise
2 tablespoons Sea Salt–Fermented Red Hot Sauce (page 247) or Crystal hot sauce
2 tablespoons Creole Mustard (page 245) or store-bought whole-grain mustard
1 teaspoon kosher salt
1 teaspoon freshly ground black pepper
1 teaspoon organic sugar

In a large bowl, combine all the ingredients and mix until well incorporated. Pack into an airtight food storage container and refrigerate for up to 7 days. We think this slaw tastes better when it has a chance to marinate overnight.

Cook Out Slaw

Makes 6–8 cups

This sweet and creamy slaw is a classic Southern favorite that's as juicy and refreshing as it is delicious. Whether enjoyed by the monkey-bowl-ful or loaded onto sandwiches, it's certain to please any crowd. Aptly named Cook Out Slaw after the revered drive-through burger joint, this recipe is our rendition of its equally fantastic slaw. So go ahead and indulge with a taste of the South in every bite. We guarantee you won't regret it.

½ head green cabbage
4 medium-to-large carrots, peeled
1 cup sour cream
¼ cup organic sugar
¼ cup apple cider vinegar
1 teaspoon celery salt
1 teaspoon freshly ground black pepper
1 cup mayonnaise

Chop the cabbage and carrots into large chunks. In a food processor, pulse half of the cabbage until finely chopped, then transfer to a large bowl. Repeat with the second half of the cabbage. Then add the carrots to the food processor, pulse until finely chopped, and add to the bowl with the cabbage.

Add the sour cream, sugar, vinegar, celery salt, and pepper to the cabbage and carrots and stir together until well mixed. Finally, fold in the mayonnaise until well mixed and the slaw is creamy. Pack into an airtight food storage container and refrigerate for up to 7 days. We think this slaw tastes better when it has a chance to marinate overnight.

Garlicky Dill Pickles

Makes ½ gallon

For over a decade, we've been perfecting the art of pickling with our tried-and-true recipe that's been served at five of our restaurants. Simple yet packed with flavor, these pickles taste even better after five days and continue to deliver for months. Just be sure to use English cucumbers to maintain that desired crunchiness. Standard garden cukes simply won't do.

3 English cucumbers, cut into ¼-inch-thick slices
2 cups water

1¼ cups distilled white vinegar
¼ cup kosher salt
¼ cup organic sugar
8 cloves garlic, smashed
2 tablespoons dried dill weed
1 tablespoon yellow mustard seeds
1 tablespoon black peppercorns
1 teaspoon red pepper flakes
2 fresh or dried bay leaves

Pack the cucumbers into a ½-gallon mason jar. In a saucepan over medium-high heat, combine the water, vinegar, salt, sugar, garlic, dill, mustard seeds, peppercorns, red pepper flakes, and bay leaves and bring to a boil. Turn down the heat to medium-low and gently simmer for 5 minutes.

Remove the pan from the heat and carefully pour the mixture into the jar with the cucumbers. Let steep uncovered at room temperature for 1 hour. Then place uncovered in the refrigerator overnight.

The next day, cap the jar. The pickles are ready to eat once fully chilled, but they will start tasting really good after 3–5 days and will keep in the refrigerator for up to 6 months.

SEASONINGS

Good seasoning is a cornerstone of great Southern cuisine. While kosher salt and freshly ground black pepper are a given, Southern cuisine typically beckons for something more complex. With so many spice blends to choose from, we've narrowed down our selection to what we reach for the most. Our Lowcountry Boil Seasoning is downright addictive, while our classic Cajun Seasoning is a linchpin for building bold flavor profiles. You won't find anything on the market quite like our jerk, rib rub, Nashville hot, or harissa, so we hope you'll take the time to make them and enjoy their rich complexities.

All of our seasonings are ready to enjoy immediately. We recommend you pack them into an airtight container (such as a mason jar) and store them in a cool, dark place (such as a pantry or cupboard not directly above your stove). Under proper storage conditions, freshly blended seasonings will remain flavorful for quite some time, but we find they taste their best when enjoyed within 6 months.

Lowcountry Boil Seasoning

Makes about 2 cups

1 bag (3 oz) Zatarain's Crawfish, Shrimp & Crab Boil
1 cup Old Bay Seasoning

Remove the spice bag from the Zatarain's box, carefully open the pouch, and finely grind its contents in a spice grinder or with a mortar and pestle. Transfer to a bowl, add the Old Bay, and mix well.

Nashville Hot Seasoning

Makes 1¼ cups

¼ cup freshly ground black pepper
¼ cup firmly packed organic dark brown sugar
¼ cup kosher salt
¼ cup smoked paprika
2 tablespoons ground chipotle chile
2 tablespoons cayenne pepper

In a bowl, whisk together all the ingredients until mixed.

Jamaican Jerk Seasoning

Makes about 2 cups

¼ cup fenugreek seeds
2 tablespoons black peppercorns
2 tablespoons cumin seeds
2 tablespoons coriander seeds
1 tablespoon green cardamom pods
1 tablespoon allspice berries
1 teaspoon whole cloves
2 tablespoons dried thyme
2 tablespoons dried oregano
¾ cup kosher salt
2 tablespoons cayenne pepper
2 tablespoons granulated garlic
2 tablespoons ground ginger
1 tablespoon ground cinnamon
1 tablespoon ground turmeric
1 tablespoon smoked paprika
1 tablespoon granulated onion
1 teaspoon ground nutmeg

Preheat a large cast-iron skillet over medium heat for 5 minutes. Add the fenugreek, peppercorns, cumin, coriander, cardamom, allspice, and cloves and dry roast, stirring frequently with a wooden spoon, until the oils in the spices begin to toast and the aroma becomes fragrant, 3–4 minutes.

Pour the roasted spices onto a sheet pan and let cool until cool to the touch, about 15 minutes. Then transfer them to a spice grinder, add the thyme and oregano, and grind until finely ground. If you have a small spice grinder, you'll need to grind the spices in batches. Transfer to a bowl. Add the salt, cayenne, garlic, ginger, cinnamon, turmeric, paprika, onion, and nutmeg and whisk together until evenly mixed.

Cajun Seasoning

Makes 1⅓ cups

¼ cup smoked paprika
¼ cup kosher salt
¼ cup granulated garlic
2 tablespoons freshly ground black pepper

2 tablespoons granulated onion

2 tablespoons cayenne pepper

2 tablespoons dried oregano

2 tablespoons dried thyme

In a bowl, whisk together all the ingredients until evenly mixed.

Coconut Rib Rub

Makes 2½ cups

1 cup coconut sugar

1 cup kosher salt

2 tablespoons dark chile powder

2 tablespoons Old Bay Seasoning

2 tablespoons cayenne pepper

2 tablespoons freshly ground black pepper

2 tablespoons granulated garlic

In a bowl, whisk together all the ingredients until evenly mixed.

Carolina Reaper Harissa

Makes about 1 cup

¼ cup Aleppo pepper flakes

2 tablespoons smoked paprika

1 tablespoon black peppercorns

1 tablespoon caraway seeds

1 tablespoon allspice berries

1 tablespoon cumin seeds

1 tablespoon coriander seeds

1 tablespoon fenugreek seeds

1 tablespoon granulated garlic

1 tablespoon kosher salt

1–3 teaspoons Carolina Reaper flakes

In a spice grinder, combine all the ingredients (adding the Carolina Reaper flakes according to the spiciness level that suits your palate) and grind until finely ground and well mixed. If you have a small spice grinder, you'll need to grind the spices in batches. Grinding seasonings together like this is a great way to unlock full flavors.

RÉMOULADES

We don't think dipping sauces should be limited to certain food groups, like fried chicken or bar fare. Seafood, be it chilled, grilled, fried, or piled high on a bun, deserves to be enjoyed with a wide variety of flavorful dipping options too.

Rémoulade, with its origin in classic French cooking, is frequently served interchangeably with tartar sauce. The main difference between the two is that the latter is often prepared straightforward—mayonnaise, pickle, herbs, and capers—while rémoulade has become regionalized by Southern kitchens. Creole rémoulade is famous throughout Louisiana, but why stop there? We've enjoyed countless variations on our travels, which eventually led to our own riffs. To us, a few key ingredients are needed to justify calling a condiment a rémoulade: mayonnaise, Creole or whole-grain mustard, raw garlic, and acid—whether from citrus, hot sauce, or both.

Our rémoulades are ready to enjoy immediately, but they taste better if allowed to sit overnight. We recommend you pack them into an airtight container (such as a mason jar) and refrigerate them immediately after mixing. Most will keep for 1 month; recipes calling for protein will have a shelf life determined by the protein used.

Creole Rémoulade

Makes 2 cups

1½ cups mayonnaise

1 tablespoon Sea Salt–Fermented Red Hot Sauce (page 247) or Crystal hot sauce

1 tablespoon peeled and finely grated fresh horseradish root, or 1 teaspoon prepared horseradish

1 tablespoon Creole Mustard (page 245) or whole-grain mustard

1 clove garlic, finely grated with a zester

½ teaspoon organic sugar

½ teaspoon kosher salt

In a bowl, whisk together all the ingredients until well mixed. Refrigerate immediately.

- Smoked Oyster Remoulade
- Lemon Garlic Remoulade
- Dill Pickle Remoulade
- Green Remoulade
- Creole Remoulade
- Red Remoulade
- Ginger Lemongrass Remoulade
- Miso Lime Remoulade

Lemon Garlic Rémoulade

Makes 2 cups

2 tablespoons Creole Mustard (page 245) or whole-grain mustard
8 cloves garlic
Grated zest and juice of 1 lemon
¼ cup avocado or canola oil
1½ cups mayonnaise
1 teaspoon freshly ground black pepper

In a food processor, combine the mustard, garlic, and lemon zest and juice and pulse until the garlic is finely chopped. With the motor running, stream in the oil and continue processing until a paste forms, stopping to scrape down the sides of the bowl if needed. Transfer the mixture to a bowl, add the mayonnaise and pepper, and mix well. Refrigerate immediately.

Red Rémoulade

Makes 2 cups

1½ cups mayonnaise
2 tablespoons ketchup
1 tablespoon Creole Mustard (page 245) or whole-grain mustard
1 tablespoon fresh lemon juice
1 tablespoon peeled and finely grated fresh horseradish root, or 1 teaspoon prepared horseradish
1 clove garlic, finely grated with a zester
1 teaspoon smoked paprika
½ teaspoon celery salt

In a bowl, whisk together all the ingredients until well mixed. Refrigerate immediately.

Green Rémoulade

Makes 2 cups

1 jalapeño chile, roughly chopped (optional)
½ poblano chile, roughly chopped
1 cup roughly chopped fresh cilantro
2 green onions, white and green parts, roughly chopped
4 cloves garlic
Grated zest and juice of ½ lime
1 tablespoon Creole Mustard (page 245) or whole-grain mustard
½ teaspoon kosher salt
1½ cups mayonnaise

In a food processor, combine the jalapeño (if using), poblano, cilantro, green onions, garlic, lime zest and juice, mustard, and salt and process until all the ingredients are finely chopped and juicy. Transfer the mixture to a bowl, add the mayonnaise, and mix well. Refrigerate immediately.

Dill Pickle Rémoulade

Makes 2 cups

1½ cups mayonnaise
⅓ cup drained and finely chopped dill pickles (preferably Grillo's)
1 tablespoon Creole Mustard (page 245) or whole-grain mustard
1 tablespoon dill pickle brine
1 tablespoon dried dill weed
1 clove garlic, finely grated with a zester
½ teaspoon freshly ground black pepper
½ teaspoon red pepper flakes

In a bowl, whisk together all the ingredients until well mixed. Refrigerate immediately.

Smoked Oyster Rémoulade

Makes 2 cups

1½ cups mayonnaise
1 can (3 oz) smoked oysters (preferably Ekone), finely chopped
1 tablespoon Creole Mustard (page 245) or whole-grain mustard
Grated zest and juice of ½ lemon
1 clove garlic, finely grated
½ teaspoon freshly ground black pepper
¼ teaspoon celery salt

In a bowl, whisk together all the ingredients until well mixed. Refrigerate immediately.

White Anchovy Rémoulade

Makes 2 cups

1½ cups mayonnaise
¼ cup drained white anchovies, finely chopped
3 tablespoons Creole Mustard (page 245) or whole-grain mustard
3 cloves garlic, finely grated with a zester
Grated zest and juice of ½ lemon
½ teaspoon freshly ground black pepper

In a bowl, whisk together all the ingredients until well mixed. Refrigerate immediately.

Calabrian Chile Rémoulade

Makes 2 cups

1½ cups mayonnaise
2 tablespoons crushed or finely chopped Calabrian chiles
1 tablespoon Creole Mustard (page 245) or whole-grain mustard
½ teaspoon smoked paprika
Grated zest and juice of ½ lemon
1 clove garlic, finely grated
½ teaspoon freshly ground black pepper

In a bowl, whisk together all the ingredients until well mixed. Refrigerate immediately.

Ginger Lemongrass Rémoulade

Makes 2 cups

1½ cups mayonnaise
1 tablespoon Creole Mustard (page 245) or whole-grain mustard
1 tablespoon peeled and finely grated fresh ginger
1 tablespoon finely grated lemongrass (bulb portion)
1 tablespoon peeled and finely grated fresh turmeric, or 1 teaspoon ground turmeric
1 clove garlic, finely grated with a zester
Grated zest and juice of ½ lime

In a bowl, whisk together all the ingredients until well mixed. Refrigerate immediately.

Miso Lime Rémoulade

Makes 2 cups

2 tablespoons red miso
1 tablespoon Sea Salt–Fermented Red Hot Sauce (page 247) or Crystal hot sauce
1 tablespoon Creole Mustard (page 245) or whole-grain mustard
1 clove garlic, finely grated with a zester
Grated zest and juice of ½ lime
1½ cups mayonnaise

In a bowl, whisk together the miso, hot sauce, mustard, garlic, and lime zest and juice until well mixed. (Miso is thick and needs to be smoothed out before the mayonnaise is added.) Add the mayonnaise and whisk until well incorporated. Refrigerate immediately.

ACCOUTREMENTS

This section offers fun, flavorful ways to accent your seafood preparations. Sure, there are plenty of options for tasty stuff on the market, but there's nothing quite like what you'll find here. We've worked on developing these recipes over the past decade. They've been staples on our menus and continue to add exciting flavor bursts to our food and dining experiences. People often tell us we should bottle them, but we figured we'd just share the recipes with y'all instead. We hope you enjoy making these as much as we do.

Chunky Creole Cocktail Sauce

Makes 2 cups

1 teaspoon fresh lemon juice
1 teaspoon Sea Salt–Fermented Red Hot Sauce (page 247) or Crystal hot sauce
½ teaspoon Worcestershire sauce
¼ red onion, roughly chopped
½ celery rib, roughly chopped
½ poblano chile, roughly chopped
1 serrano chile, roughly chopped (optional)
1 clove garlic
¼ cup peeled and finely grated fresh horseradish root, or 1 tablespoon prepared horseradish
1½ cups ketchup (preferably Sir Kensington's)
1 teaspoon freshly ground black pepper
½ teaspoon kosher salt

In a food processor, combine the lemon juice, hot sauce, Worcestershire sauce, onion, celery, poblano, serrano (if using), garlic, and horseradish and pulse until finely chopped and juicy. Transfer the mixture to a bowl, add the ketchup, pepper, and salt and whisk until well incorporated.
Transfer to an airtight container and refrigerate immediately. The sauce is ready to enjoy but tastes better if allowed to sit overnight. It will keep refrigerated for up to 1 month.

Mignonette

There's a new-school method of making mignonette that involves scaling down the acidity and straining your infused ingredients before serving, which we love. The results are crisp and clean. These mignonettes don't take away from the delicacy of an oyster. Instead, they accent it. We prefer to pack our mignonettes into dropper bottles, as they allow for a more precise dose while also eliminating waste.

Holy Trinity

1/3 cup apple cider vinegar
1/3 cup water
1 serrano chile, finely grated
1 celery rib, finely grated
2 tablespoons finely chopped red onion
1/4 teaspoon kosher salt
1/4 teaspoon organic sugar

Horseradish Garlic

1/3 cup white wine vinegar
1/3 cup water
1 clove garlic, finely grated with a zester
1 tablespoon peeled and finely grated fresh horseradish root
1/4 teaspoon kosher salt
1/4 teaspoon organic sugar

Cucumber Melon

1/3 cup distilled white vinegar
1/3 cup water
1/4 cup finely grated cucumber
1/4 cup finely grated melon, such as honeydew, watermelon, or cantaloupe
1/4 teaspoon kosher salt
1/4 teaspoon organic sugar

Mix together all the ingredients, pack into a food storage container, and refrigerate for 24 hours. Then strain through a fine-mesh sieve and transfer to a dropper bottle. Each recipe makes about 3/4 cup and will keep in the refrigerator for up to 3 months. Serve chilled on ice.

Creole Mustard

Makes 4 cups

1 cup yellow mustard seeds
1 cup brown mustard seeds
2 1/2 cups distilled white vinegar
4 cloves garlic, finely grated with a zester
1/4 cup peeled and finely grated fresh horseradish root, or 1 tablespoon prepared horseradish
2 teaspoons kosher salt

Pack all the ingredients into a 1-quart mason jar, seal tightly, and shake the jar until the contents are well mixed. Let the jar sit at room temperature until all the liquid appears to have been absorbed by the seeds. This can take 1–5 days, depending on the time of year and climate.

Pour the contents of the jar into a food processor and process until the seeds begin to crack open but are still somewhat whole and chunky, 2–3 minutes. Return the mustard to the jar, cap tightly, and refrigerate immediately. It will keep for up to 6 months.

Carolina Gold BBQ Sauce

Makes 3 cups

1/2 cup yellow mustard seeds
1 1/4 cups distilled white vinegar
1/2 cup water
1/2 cup firmly packed organic dark brown sugar
1/4 cup blackstrap molasses
1 tablespoon Worcestershire sauce
1 tablespoon liquid smoke
2 teaspoons kosher salt

Pack all the ingredients into a 1-quart mason jar, seal tightly, and shake the jar until the contents are well mixed. Let the jar sit at room temperature for 3 days.

Pour the contents of the jar into a blender and blend on high speed until smooth, about 2 minutes. While the sauce is whirling in the blender, you'll notice that the friction from the motor and blade will start to heat it up. This is good. Eventually, you'll notice steam rising from the top of the sauce. This heat allows the mustard seeds to open up fully and purée to a smooth consistency. Don't rush the process.

Every now and again, stop the blender and scrape down the sides with a rubber spatula to keep the ingredients well mixed. This technique was developed in a professional kitchen and works best when using a Vitamix blender.

Return the sauce to the jar or other airtight container, cap tightly, and refrigerate immediately. It will keep for up to 6 months.

Funky Tropical Hot Sauce

Makes 4 cups

1/2 ripe banana, peeled and sliced 1/4 inch thick
1/2 ripe mango, peeled and sliced 1/4 inch thick
4 oz habanero chiles, sliced 1/4 inch thick
2 oz jalapeño chiles, sliced 1/4 inch thick
2 oz serrano chiles, sliced 1/4 inch thick
3 tablespoons kosher salt
1 tablespoon sugar
1 cup distilled white vinegar
1 cup water, or as needed

Firmly pack the banana, mango, and all the chiles into a 1-quart mason jar. Add the salt, sugar, vinegar, and water. If needed, top off with water so the jar is filled to the top and all the ingredients are submerged. Seal tightly and shake the jar hard until the salt and sugar dissolve, about 1 minute. Let the contents of the jar pickle in a cool, dark place for 4–7 days. The time it needs to pickle will depend on the time of year, location, temperature, and humidity. A good rule of thumb is that the hotter it is, the less time it will take for the flavors to develop. Essentially, you are shelf pickling the chiles in this step, which imparts a pleasantly piquant profile to the finished sauce.

Pour the contents of the jar into a blender and blend on high speed until the mixture is as smooth as possible, about 2 minutes. Pour through a fine-mesh sieve placed over a bowl to remove any pulp, using a spoon in a scraping motion to help pass the sauce through the sieve.

Transfer the sauce to sterilized jars or bottles of your choice, cap tightly, and refrigerate for up to 1 year. Shake well before each use.

Bourbon Barrel–Aged Green Hot Sauce

Makes 4 cups

1 lb jalapeño chiles, sliced 1/4 inch thick
3 tablespoons kosher salt
1 1/2 tablespoons organic sugar
1 cup distilled white vinegar
3/4 cup water
1 tablespoon bourbon (preferably Knob Creek)
1 cup bourbon barrel smoking chips (preferably Knob Creek)

Firmly pack the chiles into a sterilized 1-quart mason jar. Add the salt, sugar, vinegar, water, and bourbon. If needed, top off with water so the jar is filled to the top and all the chiles are submerged. Seal tightly and shake the jar hard until the salt and sugar dissolve, about 1 minute. Let the contents of the jar pickle in a cool, dark place for 4–7 days. The time it needs to pickle will depend on the time of year, location, temperature, and humidity. A good rule of thumb is that the hotter it is, the less time it will take for the flavors to develop. Essentially, you are shelf pickling the chiles in this step, which imparts a pleasantly piquant profile to the finished sauce.

Pour the contents of the jar into a blender and blend on high speed until the mixture is as smooth as possible, about 2 minutes. Pour through a fine-mesh sieve placed over a bowl to remove any pulp, using a spoon in a scraping motion to help pass the sauce through the sieve. If you aren't taking the additional step to infuse your hot sauce with bourbon barrel chips, skip to the last step.

To simulate barrel aging at home, put the smoking chips into a bowl, rinse well to remove any debris or dust, and then drain well. Add the chips and the strained hot sauce to a sterilized 1-quart mason jar, seal tightly, and shake hard for 1 minute. Now allow the sauce to steep in a cool, dark place for 7 days, shaking the jar once a day to maximize barrel-flavor extraction. Although you aren't barrel aging, you are imparting the flavors of the toasted wood and bourbon by means of infusion. This is a technique we learned from the wine industry. At the end of 7 days, strain the sauce through the fine-mesh sieve to remove the barrel chips.

Transfer the sauce to sterilized jars or bottles of your choice, cap tightly, and refrigerate for up to 1 year. Shake well before each use.

Sea-Salt–Fermented Red Hot Sauce

Makes 4 cups

Fermented vegetable condiments aren't just full of flavor and gut-healthy probiotics. They're a time-honored method of preserving spring and summer harvests (in anticipation of winter) that predates modern refrigeration. We see them a lot in ancient cultures—think Korean kimchi. But did you know that fermentation has been heavily relied on by Southerners since the early days of settlement? And it's not just limited to vegetables. That country ham biscuit you crave every Saturday morning wouldn't be possible without a hefty dose of salt and the subtropical highland climate of Southern Appalachia.

Most of the fermentation culture in the South has roots in the Appalachian Mountains region, where colder winters made preserving foods critical for survival. The area also provides ideal temperatures and humidity levels for fermenting everything from chowchow and piccalilli to bourbon whiskey and country ham. No matter how many times we preserve foods, it simply amazes us that the planet provides us with all the tools we need.

One of the most dynamic attributes of fermentation is its broad range of flavor development. Keep that in mind when determining how long you let this hot sauce ferment. A young or just fermented hot sauce will be quite vibrant, fruity, and spicy, with just a touch of tang, while a longer-aged hot sauce will begin to mellow the capsaicin heat and take on the funkier flavors of fermentation (which are heavily dictated by the billions of microbes native to your local climate).

Caution is advised. Going too long can result in the growth of undesirable bacteria or fungus, ruining your batch. We recommend starting off with something a little younger and getting the basics down. From there, as time goes on and you gain experience with fermenting in your household throughout the seasons, you can make more informed decisions on how long to let controlled rot take place. Eventually, you can get into open-air or even barrel-aged fermentation.

6 oz red Fresno chiles, sliced ¼ inch thick
3 oz carrot, peeled and sliced ¼ inch thick (about ¾ cup)
2 oz Vidalia or other sweet onion, sliced ¼ inch thick (about ¾ cup)
½ oz garlic, sliced ¼ inch thick (about 3 cloves)
2 tablespoons plus 2 teaspoons flaky sea salt
2 tablespoons organic sugar
2 cups water

Firmly pack the chiles, carrot, onion, and garlic into a sterilized 1-quart mason jar. Add the salt, sugar, and water, seal tightly, and shake the jar hard until the salt and sugar dissolve, about 1 minute. Loosen the lid to a half seal so any potential gas can escape. Let the contents of the jar ferment in a cool, dark place for 4–7 days. This use of a salt-and-sugar water brine with no vinegar is known as lacto-fermentation. Essentially, you're allowing good local bacteria to break down sugars and form lactic acid, yielding a funkier profile with probiotics and an extended shelf life. The time it needs to ferment will depend on the time of year, location, temperature, and humidity. A good rule of thumb is that the hotter it is, the faster the fermentation will start. We like to start looking for signs of fermentation on day two, but we don't typically expect to see them until day four or five. What you're looking for is the presence of tiny bubbles and the emergence of a cloudy brine. Once you've discovered signs of fermentation, you have two options: move on to the next step or allow the fermentation process to continue.

When the desired level of fermentation has been achieved, pour the contents of the jar into a blender and blend on high speed until the mixture is as smooth as possible, about 2 minutes. Pour through a fine-mesh sieve placed over a bowl to remove any pulp, using a spoon in a scraping motion to help pass the sauce through the sieve.

Transfer the sauce to sterilized jars or bottles of your choice, cap tightly, and refrigerate for up to 1 year. Shake well before each use.

INDEX

A

Ají Amarillo, Fluke Ceviche with, 51
Aleppo pepper flakes
    Carolina Reaper Harissa, 241
Algae
    about, 25
    Blue Bayou, 22
    toxic blooms, 220
    types of, 25
All Clams on Deck, 220
Amberjack Crudo, Gulf Coast, 54–55
Anchored Shrimp Co., 129
Ancho Syrup, 26
Anson Mills, 147, 216
Aperol
    Texas Two-Timer, 28
Avocados
    Pineapple Guac, 105
    Yellowfin Tuna & Watermelon Salad, 68

B

Backyard Charleston Oyster Roast, 205–6
Backyard shellfish boils, 138–40
Bacon & Beer Braised Clams, 170
Bananas
    Funky Tropical Hot Sauce, 246
Barbecued Grouper Cheeks, Carolina Gold, 198
Barbecued Pompano, Coconut Unagi, 214–15
Basil
    Nuoc Cham Crab Salad, 67
    Yellowfin Tuna & Watermelon Salad, 68
Batter, Beer, Light & Crispy, 149
BBQ Sauce, Carolina Gold, 245–46
Beans
    Wahoo Brunswick Stew, 136
    Whole Snapper with Autumn Succotash, 167
Beer
    Bacon & Beer Braised Clams, 170
    Light & Crispy Beer Batter, 149

Benne seeds
    about, 216
    Cajun Dukkah, 200
    Pecan Salsa Macha, 202
    Romesco, 200–201
Blackened Fish, Perfectly, 183
Blackened Redfish Tacos with Hoppin' John Salsa, 116–17
Black-eyed peas
    Hoppin' John Salsa, 117
Black pepper
    Cacio e Pepe Grits, 237
    Nashville Hot Seasoning, 239
Black Sea Bass Escabeche, Salt-Crusted, 223–24
Bloody Mary mix
    Captain Creole, 35
    Shrunken Head(ache), 36
Blue Bayou, 22
Blue spirulina
    Blue Bayou, 22
    health benefits, 25
Bonefish, North Carolina, about, 152
Bottarga, about, 98
Bourbon
    Bourbon Barrel-Aged Green Hot Sauce, 246
    Savannah Slush, 39
Brandy
    Caddywampus Punch, 40
    Strawberry Brandy, 40
Bread. See also Toast
    Lowcountry Cast-Iron Corn Bread, 233
    Savory Oyster Bread Pudding, 184
Breading for frying
    Calabash Style, 145
    Carolina Cornmeal, 146
    Panko Crunch, 150
Brunswick Stew, Wahoo, 136
Butter
    Peanut Chile Crisp–Butter Shrimp, 86
    Whipped Green Chile Butter, 81
Buttermilk
    Calabash Style Breading, 145
    Carolina Cornmeal Breading, 146
    Savannah-Style Cobia Crudo, 52

C

Cabbage
    Cook Out Slaw, 238
    Pop's Slaw, 238
Cacio e Pepe Grits, 237
Cajun Dukkah, 200
Cajun Fried Saltines, 176
Cajun Lobster Cocktail, 64
Cajun Seasoning, 240–41
Cajun Yuca Steak Fries, 154
Calabash Style Breading, 145
Calabash-Style Rock Shrimp Sandwich, 121
Candied Yams, Extra-Fancy, 230
Captain Creole, 35
Caribbean Spiny Lobster Mulitas, 104–5
Carolina Cherry Crush, 29
Carolina Cornmeal Breading, 146
Carolina corn revival, 147
Carolina Gold BBQ Sauce, 245–46
Carolina Reaper Harissa, 241
Carolina-Style Colossal Shrimp Cocktail, 63
Carrots
    Cook Out Slaw, 238
    Mahi-Mahi Curry Pot, 179
    Sea-Salt Fermented Red Hot Sauce, 247
Cast-iron cookware, 162, 165, 180
Catfish
    Catfish & Country Ham Croquetas, 82–83
    Harissa Charred Catfish, 196–97
Caviar service, proper, 61
Ceviche
    about, 50
    Creole Bay Scallop Ceviche, 48
    Fluke Ceviche with Ají Amarillo, 51
    Gulf Coast Amberjack Crudo, 54–55
    Savannah-Style Cobia Crudo, 52
Charleston Oyster Roast, Backyard, 205–6
Charleston Perloo, 133–34
Cheese
    Cacio e Pepe Grits, 237

Caribbean Spiny Lobster
    Mulitas, 104–5
Crab Gratin en Cocotte with
    Cajun Fried Saltines, 176
Crab & Green Chile Pimento
    Cheese, 85
Crawfish & Tasso Mac 'n' Cheese, 168
Fish Shack Double Stack Deluxe, 110
Oyster Bed Bienville with
    Texas Toast, 227
Swordfish Cubano, 102–3
Cherry Crush, Carolina, 29
Chile Crisp, Peanut, 86
Chiles
    Ancho Syrup, 26
    Bourbon Barrel-Aged Green
        Hot Sauce, 246
    Calabrian Chile Rémoulade, 244
    Crab & Green Chile Pimento
        Cheese, 85
    Creole Bay Scallop Ceviche, 48
    Fluke Ceviche with Ají Amarillo, 51
    Funky Tropical Hot Sauce, 246
    Holy Trinity Mignonette, 245
    Key West Pink Shrimp
        Aguachile, 56–57
    Pecan Salsa Macha, 202
    Poblano Vodka, 35
    Romesco, 200–201
    Salt-Crusted Black Sea Bass
        Escabeche, 223–24
    Sea-Salt Fermented Red
        Hot Sauce, 247
    Whipped Green Chile Butter, 81
Chimichurri, Collard Green, 55
Chlorella
    health benefits, 25
    Pawleys Island Palmer, 45
Chowder, Smoked Oyster &
    Butternut Squash, 137
Cilantro
    Blood Orange Mojo, 103
    Collard Green Chimichurri, 55
    Green Rémoulade, 243
    Key West Pink Shrimp
        Aguachile, 56–57
    Nuoc Cham Crab Salad, 67
    Romesco, 200–201
    Sweet & Spicy Fish Collars, 209
    Yellowfin Tuna & Watermelon
        Salad, 68

Citrus. See also specific citrus fruits
    dehydrated, preparing, 27
Clams
    Bacon & Beer Braised Clams, 170
    Floribbean Clam Boil, 140
    Jamaican Jerk Conch Fritters, 79
    from Sapelo Sea Farms, 171
    Topneck Clams al Forno, 219
Cobia
    Fish Shack Double Stack Deluxe, 110
    Savannah-Style Cobia Crudo, 52
Cocktails
    Blue Bayou, 22
    Caddywampus Punch, 40
    Captain Creole, 35
    Hibiscus Hoodoo, 18
    Lowcountry Cure, 42
    Mezcalarita del Diablo, 26
    Punk Evans, 21
    Savannah Slush, 39
    Shrunken Head(ache), 36
    Texas Two-Timer, 28
    Voodoo Queen, 32
    The Whisky Thief, 31
Cocktail Sauce, Chunky Creole, 244
Coconut
    Coconut Rib Rub, 241
    Coconut Unagi Barbecued
        Pompano, 214–15
    Houston Hoedown, 43
Coconut milk
    Coconut Ginger Collards, 235
    Lowcountry Cure, 42
    Mahi-Mahi Curry Pot, 179
Cointreau
    Mezcalarita del Diablo, 26
    Punk Evans, 21
Collard greens
    Coconut Ginger Collards, 235
    Collard Green Chimichurri, 55
    Pop's Slaw, 238
Conch Fritters, Jamaican Jerk, 79
Cook Out Slaw, 238
Corn
    Floribbean Clam Boil, 140
    Gullah Geechee Crab Fried Rice, 173
    heirloom varieties, 147
    Louisiana Crawfish Boil, 140
    Lowcountry Shrimp Boil, 140
    Wahoo Brunswick Stew, 136

Whole Snapper with Autumn
    Succotash, 167
Corn Bread, Lowcountry Cast-Iron, 233
Cornmeal
    Carolina Cornmeal Breading, 146
    Louisiana Crawfish
        Hushpuppies, 80–81
    Lowcountry Cast-Iron
        Corn Bread, 233
    North Carolina–Style
        Hushpuppies, 159
Costco, 15
Crab
    Crab Gratin en Cocotte with
        Cajun Fried Saltines, 176
    Crab & Green Chile Pimento
        Cheese, 85
    Extra-Fancy Crab Cakes, 175
    Gullah Geechee Crab Fried Rice, 173
    Nuoc Cham Crab Salad, 67
Crawfish
    Crawfish & Tasso Mac 'n' Cheese, 168
    Louisiana Crawfish Boil, 140
    from Louisiana Crawfish
        Company, 115
    Louisiana Crawfish
        Hushpuppies, 80–81
    Louisiana Crawfish Roll, 113
Creole Bay Scallop Ceviche, 48
Creole Cocktail Sauce, Chunky, 244
Creole Mustard, 245
Creole Rémoulade, 241
Croquetas, Catfish & Country
    Ham, 82–83
Cucumbers
    Cucumber Melon Mignonette, 245
    Cucumber Syrup, 31
    Fluke Ceviche with Ají Amarillo, 51
    Garlicky Dill Pickles, 238–39
    Key West Pink Shrimp
        Aguachile, 56–57
    Yellowfin Tuna & Watermelon
        Salad, 68
Curry Pot, Mahi-Mahi, 179

D

Deviled Eggs, Sunburst
    Smoked Trout, 97
Dill Pickle Rémoulade, 243
Dill Pickles, Garlicky, 238–39

Dips
  Crab Gratin en Cocotte with
    Cajun Fried Saltines, 176
  Smoked Mackerel Dip, 93
Drinks. *See also Cocktails*
  Carolina Cherry Crush, 29
  Houston Hoedown, 43
  Lowcountry Cure, 42
  Pawleys Island Palmer, 45
Dukkah, Cajun, 200

E
Eco certifications, 14
Eggs
  Smoked Trout & Sweet
    Potato Hash, 187
  Sunburst Smoked Trout
    Deviled Eggs, 97
Escabeche, Salt-Crusted Black
  Sea Bass, 223–24

F
Falernum
  Voodoo Queen, 32
Fenugreek seeds
  Jamaican Jerk Seasoning, 240
Fish
  Blackened Redfish Tacos with
    Hoppin' John Salsa, 116–17
  Carolina Gold Barbecued
    Grouper Cheeks, 198
  Catfish & Country Ham
    Croquetas, 82–83
  Coconut Unagi Barbecued
    Pompano, 214–15
  Extra-Fancy Crab Cakes, 175
  Fish 'n' Chips Submarine, 109
  Fish Shack Double Stack Deluxe, 110
  fish-smoking technique, 213
  Fluke Ceviche with Ají Amarillo, 51
  frying chart, 144
  Gulf Coast Amberjack Crudo, 54–55
  Harissa Charred Catfish, 196–97
  Hickory-Roasted Monkfish
    Veracruzana, 194
  Mahi-Mahi Curry Pot, 179
  The Miami, 107
  North Carolina bonefish, about, 152
  Perfectly Blackened Fish, 183
  Salt-Crusted Black Sea Bass
    Escabeche, 223–24
  Savannah-Style Cobia Crudo, 52
  Smoked Bluehouse Salmon
    Bravas, 211–12
  Smoked Mackerel Dip, 93
  Smoked Trout & Sweet
    Potato Hash, 187
  Spicy Swordfish and Chorizo
    Meatballs, 99
  Sunburst Smoked Trout
    Deviled Eggs, 97
  sustainably caught tuna, 69
  Sweet & Spicy Fish Collars, 209
  Swordfish Cubano, 102–3
  Tilefish with Pecan Salsa
    Macha, 202–3
  tinned fish, buying, 94
  Wahoo Brunswick Stew, 136
  White Anchovy Rémoulade, 243
  White Wine Fish Stock, 135
  Whole Snapper with Autumn
    Succotash, 167
  Wreckfish a la Parrilla, 200–201
  Yellowfin Tuna & Watermelon
    Salad, 68
Fish camps, 143
Fish roe
  bottarga, about, 98
  proper caviar service, 61
  Smoked Mackerel Dip, 93
Floribbean Clam Boil, 140
Fluke Ceviche with Ají Amarillo, 51
Fontana Forni, 217
Fries
  Cajun Yuca Steak Fries, 154
  Fish 'n' Chips Submarine, 109
Fritters
  Jamaican Jerk Conch Fritters, 79
  Louisiana Crawfish
    Hushpuppies, 80–81
  North Carolina–Style
    Hushpuppies, 159
Fruit. *See also specific fruits*
  dehydrated citrus, preparing, 27
  Funky Tropical Hot Sauce, 246
Frying chart, 144

G
Garlic
  Blood Orange Mojo, 103
  Collard Green Chimichurri, 55
  Garlicky Dill Pickles, 238–39
  Horseradish Garlic Mignonette, 245
  Lemon Garlic Rémoulade, 243
George & Pink's, 236
Gin
  Hibiscus Hoodoo, 18
Ginger
  Coconut Ginger Collards, 235
  Ginger Lemongrass Rémoulade, 244
  Lemongrass-Ginger Syrup, 21
  Mahi-Mahi Curry Pot, 179
Grain mills, 147
Green Rémoulade, 243
Grilling
  with hardwood, 193
  on pellet grills, 208
Grits
  Cacio e Pepe Grits, 237
  Lowcountry Shrimp & Grits, 127
Grouper
  Carolina Gold Barbecued
    Grouper Cheeks, 198
  The Miami, 107
Guac, Pineapple, 105
Gulf Coast Amberjack Crudo, 54–55
Gullah Geechee community, 172
Gullah Geechee Crab Fried Rice, 173
Gumbo
  about, 131
  Shellfish Gumbo Pot, 130

H
Ham
  Catfish & Country Ham
    Croquetas, 82–83
  Crawfish & Tasso Mac 'n' Cheese, 168
  Swordfish Cubano, 102–3
Hardwood, cooking with, 191–93
Harissa
  about, 197
  Carolina Reaper Harissa, 241
  Harissa Charred Catfish, 196–97
Hash, Smoked Trout &
  Sweet Potato, 187
Herbs. *See Basil; Cilantro; Dill;*
  Mint; Parsley; Sage
Hibiscus Hoodoo, 18
Hibiscus Syrup, 18
Hickory-Roasted Monkfish
  Veracruzana, 194
Holy Trinity Mignonette, 245
Hominy
  Whole Snapper with Autumn
    Succotash, 167
Hoppin' John Salsa, 117

Horseradish Garlic Mignonette, 245
Hot sauce
    Bourbon Barrel-Aged Green Hot Sauce, 246
    Funky Tropical Hot Sauce, 246
    Sea-Salt Fermented Red Hot Sauce, 247
Houston Hoedown, 43
Hushpuppies
    Louisiana Crawfish Hushpuppies, 80–81
    North Carolina–Style Hushpuppies, 159

I
Ice cubes
    Lime Ice Cubes, 29
    Watermelon Ice Cubes, 21

J
Jamaican Jerk Seasoning, 240
Jamaican Jerk Tostones, 155

K
Key West Pink Shrimp Aguachile, 56–57
Korean chile flakes
    Peanut Chile Crisp, 86
Kumquats
    Blue Bayou, 22
    Houston Hoedown, 43

L
Lavender-Sage Syrup, 45
Lemon
    dehydrated, preparing, 27
    Gulf Coast Amberjack Crudo, 54–55
    Lemon Garlic Rémoulade, 243
    Pawleys Island Palmer, 45
Lemongrass
    Ginger Lemongrass Rémoulade, 244
    Lemongrass-Ginger Syrup, 21
Lime
    dehydrated, preparing, 27
    Gulf Coast Amberjack Crudo, 54–55
    Lime Ice Cubes, 29
    Lowcountry Cure, 42
    Miso Lime Rémoulade, 244
Lobster
    Cajun Lobster Cocktail, 64
    Caribbean Spiny Lobster Mulitas, 104–5
    Lobster Rémoulade–Stuffed Piquillo Peppers, 90

Louisiana Crawfish Boil, 140
Louisiana Crawfish Company, 115
Louisiana Crawfish Hushpuppies, 80–81
Louisiana Crawfish Roll, 113
Lowcountry Boil Seasoning, 239
Lowcountry Cast-Iron Corn Bread, 233
Lowcountry Cure, 42
Lowcountry Shrimp Boil, 140
Lowcountry Shrimp & Grits, 127

M
Mackerel, Smoked, Dip, 93
Mac 'n' Cheese, Crawfish & Tasso, 168
Mahi-Mahi Curry Pot, 179
Mango
    Funky Tropical Hot Sauce, 246
    Savannah Slush, 39
Meatballs, Spicy Swordfish and Chorizo, 99
Melon
    Cucumber Melon Mignonette, 245
    Watermelon Ice Cubes, 21
    Yellowfin Tuna & Watermelon Salad, 68
Mezcal
    Mezcalarita del Diablo, 26
The Miami, 107
Mignonette, 245
Mint
    Nuoc Cham Crab Salad, 67
    Yellowfin Tuna & Watermelon Salad, 68
Miso Lime Rémoulade, 244
Mojo, Blood Orange, 103
Monkfish, Hickory-Roasted, Veracruzana, 194
Mulitas, Caribbean Spiny Lobster, 104–5
Murder Point Oysters, 71
Mussels
    Marinated Mussels Toast, 89
    Shellfish Gumbo Pot, 130
Mustard
    Carolina Gold BBQ Sauce, 245–46
    Creole Mustard, 245

N
Nashville Hot Seasoning, 239
Nongovernmental organizations (NGOs), 15
North Carolina bonefish, about, 152
North Carolina–Style Hushpuppies, 159

Nuoc Cham Crab Salad, 67
Nuts. *See also* Peanuts
    Pecan Salsa Macha, 202

O
Okra
    Shellfish Gumbo Pot, 130
    Wahoo Brunswick Stew, 136
Olives
    Hickory-Roasted Monkfish Veracruzana, 194
Onions
    Holy Trinity Mignonette, 245
    Pickled Red Onion, 55
    Sea-Salt Fermented Red Hot Sauce, 247
Oranges
    Blood Orange Mojo, 103
    dehydrated, preparing, 27
    Gulf Coast Amberjack Crudo, 54–55
Orgeat
    Caddywampus Punch, 40
    Voodoo Queen, 32
Oysters
    Backyard Charleston Oyster Roast, 205–6
    Charleston Perloo, 133–34
    Fully Dressed Oyster Po'Boy, 119
    information sources, 75
    Oyster Bed Bienville with Texas Toast, 227
    salinity levels, 74
    Savory Oyster Bread Pudding, 184
    scrubbing and storing, 73
    Shellfish Gumbo Pot, 130
    shucking and serving, 73–74
    Smoked Oyster & Butternut Squash Chowder, 137
    Smoked Oyster Rémoulade, 243
    sourcing, 70–73
Oyster South, 75

P
Panko Crunch, 150
Paprika
    Cajun Seasoning, 240–41
    Carolina Reaper Harissa, 241
    Nashville Hot Seasoning, 239
Parsley
    Romesco, 200–201
    Smoked Mackerel Dip, 93

Sunburst Smoked Trout
    Deviled Eggs, 97
Passion fruit
    Shrunken Head(ache), 36
    Texas Two-Timer, 28
Pasta. *See* Mac 'n' Cheese
Pawleys Island Palmer, 45
Peaches
    Savannah Slush, 39
    Savannah-Style Cobia Crudo, 52
Peanuts
    Cajun Dukkah, 200
    Peanut Chile Crisp, 86
    Romesco, 200–201
Peas
    Hoppin' John Salsa, 117
    Pepsi-Cola Sea Island Red Peas, 234
Pecan Salsa Macha, 202
Pellet grills, 208
Peppers. *See also* Chiles
    Hickory-Roasted Monkfish
        Veracruzana, 194
    Lobster Rémoulade–Stuffed
        Piquillo Peppers, 90
    Salt-Crusted Black Sea Bass
        Escabeche, 223–24
Pepsi-Cola Sea Island Red Peas, 234
Perloo, Charleston, 133–34
Pickled Red Onion, 55
Pickles
    Dill Pickle Rémoulade, 243
    Garlicky Dill Pickles, 238–39
Pimento Cheese, Crab & Green Chile, 85
Pineapple
    Pineapple Guac, 105
    Pineapple Vodka, 36
Pin Point Heritage Museum, 172
Plantains
    Jamaican Jerk Tostones, 155
    Mahi-Mahi Curry Pot, 179
Poblano Vodka, 35
Po'Boy, Oyster, Fully Dressed, 119
Pompano, Coconut Unagi
    Barbecued, 214–15
Pork. *See* Bacon; Ham; Sausage
Potatoes
    Catfish & Country Ham
        Croquetas, 82–83
    Chip Shop Scalloped Potatoes, 58
    Fish 'n' Chips Submarine, 109
    Floribbean Clam Boil, 140

Louisiana Crawfish Boil, 140
Lowcountry Shrimp Boil, 140
Smoked Trout & Sweet
    Potato Hash, 187
Wahoo Brunswick Stew, 136
Pudding, Savory Oyster Bread, 184
Punch, Caddywampus, 40
Punk Evans, 21
Purveyors, credible, 15

R

Raspberries
    Houston Hoedown, 43
Recteq pellet grills, 208
Redfish, Blackened, Tacos with
    Hoppin' John Salsa, 116–17
Red Rémoulade, 243
Red tides, 220
Rémoulades
    about, 241
    Calabrian Chile Rémoulade, 244
    Creole Rémoulade, 241
    Dill Pickle Rémoulade, 243
    Ginger Lemongrass Rémoulade, 244
    Green Rémoulade, 243
    Lemon Garlic Rémoulade, 243
    Miso Lime Rémoulade, 244
    Red Rémoulade, 243
    Smoked Oyster Rémoulade, 243
    White Anchovy Rémoulade, 243
Rib Rub, Coconut, 241
Rice
    Charleston Perloo, 133–34
    Gullah Geechee Crab Fried Rice, 173
    Seared Sea Scallops with
        Middlins, 188
Romesco, 200–201
Rum
    Blue Bayou, 22
    Voodoo Queen, 32

S

Sage-Lavender Syrup, 45
Salads
    Nuoc Cham Crab Salad, 67
    Yellowfin Tuna & Watermelon
        Salad, 68
Salinity, in oysters, 74
Salmon Bravas, Smoked
    Bluehouse, 211–12
Salsa
    Hoppin' John Salsa, 117
    Pecan Salsa Macha, 202

Salt-Crusted Black Sea Bass
    Escabeche, 223–24
Saltines, Cajun Fried, 176
Sandwiches
    Calabash-Style Rock Shrimp
        Sandwich, 121
    Fish 'n' Chips Submarine, 109
    Fish Shack Double Stack Deluxe, 110
    Fully Dressed Oyster Po'Boy, 119
    Louisiana Crawfish Roll, 113
    The Miami, 107
    Swordfish Cubano, 102–3
Sapelo Sea Farms, 171
Sauces. *See also* Rémoulades
    Bourbon Barrel-Aged Green
        Hot Sauce, 246
    Carolina Gold BBQ Sauce, 245–46
    Chunky Creole Cocktail Sauce, 244
    Collard Green Chimichurri, 55
    Creole Mustard, 245
    Funky Tropical Hot Sauce, 246
    Mignonette, 245
    Pecan Salsa Macha, 202
    Romesco, 200–201
    Sea-Salt Fermented Red
        Hot Sauce, 247
Sausage
    Charleston Perloo, 133–34
    Floribbean Clam Boil, 140
    Louisiana Crawfish Boil, 140
    Lowcountry Shrimp Boil, 140
    Spicy Swordfish and Chorizo
        Meatballs, 99
    Topneck Clams al Forno, 219
Savannah Slush, 39
Savannah-Style Cobia Crudo, 52
Scallops
    Creole Bay Scallop Ceviche, 48
    Seared Sea Scallops with
        Middlins, 188
Seafood Watch, 14–15, 69
Seagrass meadows, 220
Sea Island Forge kettles, 207
Sea Island Red Peas, Pepsi-Cola, 234
Sea Love Sea Salt, 38
Sea-Salt Fermented Red Hot Sauce, 247
Seasonings
    Cajun Seasoning, 240–41
    Carolina Reaper Harissa, 241
    Coconut Rib Rub, 241
    Jamaican Jerk Seasoning, 240
    Lowcountry Boil Seasoning, 239

Nashville Hot Seasoning, 239
Shellfish. *See also* Crab; Crawfish; Mussels; Oysters; Scallops; Shrimp
  backyard shellfish boils, 138–40
  Cajun Lobster Cocktail, 64
  Caribbean Spiny Lobster Mulitas, 104–5
  frying chart, 144
  Jamaican Jerk Conch Fritters, 79
  Lobster Rémoulade–Stuffed Piquillo Peppers, 90
  Pan-Roasted Shellfish Stock, 124
Shrimp
  from Anchored Shrimp Co., 129
  Calabash-Style Rock Shrimp Sandwich, 121
  Carolina-Style Colossal Shrimp Cocktail, 63
  Charleston Perloo, 133–34
  Key West Pink Shrimp Aguachile, 56–57
  Lowcountry Shrimp Boil, 140
  Lowcountry Shrimp & Grits, 127
  Peanut Chile Crisp–Butter Shrimp, 86
  quality, sourcing, 134
  Shellfish Gumbo Pot, 130
  from Sun Shrimp, 88
Shrunken Head(ache), 36
Simple Syrup, 22
Slaws
  Cook Out Slaw, 238
  Pop's Slaw, 238
Smithey Ironware, 180
Smoking fish, 213
Snapper
  Fish 'n' Chips Submarine, 109
  Whole Snapper with Autumn Succotash, 167
Sodium tripolyphosphate (STPP), 134
Southern oyster farms, 71
Squash
  Smoked Oyster & Butternut Squash Chowder, 137
  Whole Snapper with Autumn Succotash, 167
Stews
  gumbo, about, 131
  Shellfish Gumbo Pot, 130
  Wahoo Brunswick Stew, 136
Stocks
  All-Purpose Backyard Boil Stock, 139
  Pan-Roasted Shellfish Stock, 124
  White Wine Fish Stock, 135
Strawberries
  Caddywampus Punch, 40
  Strawberry Brandy, 40
Succotash, Autumn, Whole Snapper with, 167
Sunburst Trout Farms, 97
Sun Shrimp, 88
Sustainability ratings, 14–15
Sustainable seafood, 13–15, 69, 71, 115, 171, 220
Sweet Potato & Smoked Trout Hash, 187
Swordfish
  Spicy Swordfish and Chorizo Meatballs, 99
  Swordfish Cubano, 102–3
Syrups
  Ancho Syrup, 26
  Cucumber Syrup, 31
  Hibiscus Syrup, 18
  Lavender-Sage Syrup, 45
  Lemongrass-Ginger Syrup, 21
  Simple Syrup, 22

T
Tacos, Blackened Redfish, with Hoppin' John Salsa, 116–17
Tea
  Pawleys Island Palmer, 45
Tequila
  Texas Two-Timer, 28
Texas Two-Timer, 28
Tilefish with Pecan Salsa Macha, 202–3
Tinned fish, buying, 94
Toadfish oyster knives, 73
Toast
  Marinated Mussels Toast, 89
  Oyster Bed Bienville with Texas Toast, 227
Tomatoes
  Fluke Ceviche with Ají Amarillo, 51
  Harissa Charred Catfish, 196–97
  Hickory-Roasted Monkfish Veracruzana, 194
  Marinated Mussels Toast, 89
  Smoked Bluehouse Salmon Bravas, 211–12
  Spicy Swordfish and Chorizo Meatballs, 99
  Wahoo Brunswick Stew, 136
Tortillas
  Blackened Redfish Tacos with Hoppin' John Salsa, 116–17
  Caribbean Spiny Lobster Mulitas, 104–5
Tostones, Jamaican Jerk, 155
Trout
  Smoked Trout & Sweet Potato Hash, 187
  Sunburst Smoked Trout Deviled Eggs, 97
Tuna
  sustainably caught, 69
  Yellowfin Tuna & Watermelon Salad, 68

V
Vodka
  Captain Creole, 35
  Pineapple Vodka, 36
  Poblano Vodka, 35
  Punk Evans, 21
  Shrunken Head(ache), 36
Voodoo Queen, 32

W
Wahoo Brunswick Stew, 136
Watermelon
  Watermelon Ice Cubes, 21
  Yellowfin Tuna & Watermelon Salad, 68
The Whisky Thief, 31
White Anchovy Rémoulade, 243
Whole Foods, 15
Wine
  Hibiscus Hoodoo, 18
  White Wine Fish Stock, 135
Wood-fired oven cookery, 217
Wreckfish a la Parrilla, 200–201

Y
Yams
  Extra-Fancy Candied Yams, 230
  Mahi-Mahi Curry Pot, 179
Yuca Steak Fries, Cajun, 154

ACKNOWLEDGEMENTS

Much more than a handful of howdy-dos and a mouthful of much obliged go to . . .

Our family we can't seem to get rid of, our friends whom we don't want to, and all those fine folks we've met along this journey that we now call friends. Without their support, feedback, generosity, knowledge, help, connections, kindness, and love, we would have had much less success than we did writing this cookbook.

To family and friends: Debby & Sam Monsour, Michele Black, David Black, Devan Yates, Brian Wiggins, Steve Wiggins, Jenny Wolfe & Ben Fulton, Jon Black & Olivia Hipp, Laney Black, Lendy Black; Kimberly & Enzo & Dante di Bonaventura, Sheila Bowman, Shaun Brian, Steph Burt, Ed Chiles, Chris Coombs, Damian Diaz, William Dissen, Ashley Erwin, Devon Espinosa & Robbie Joseph, Bianca Gouahoury, Chris Guarino, Esther & Neal Hodges, Sammy Jackson, Katie & Teddy Lee, Ruth Driscoll-Lovejoy, Molly McGaughey-Lee, Trey McMillian, Ricky Moore, Melissa Flores & Othon Nolasco, Daren Palacios, Laura & Corey Peet, Steve Phelps, Chris Pircher, Barton Seaver, Jeff Sedeca, Sandy & Steve Schoettle, Jacob Schiffman, Barton Seaver, TaMiya Dickerson & Joel Stallworth, Clint & Camille Strickland, Chris Strickland, Amber & Brandon Stover, Maddie Voorhees, Leigh-Kathryn & Jeremy Wall, Lane Zirlott.

To the establishments that fed us along the way of our two-year travels and generously showed us Southern hospitality: Adams Street Grocery, Amara at Paraiso, Anchored Shrimp Co., A. P. Bell Fish Co., B & B Seafood, Bacchanal, Bellwether House, Buffa's, Captain Jim's Seafood, Central Grocery, Common Thread, Compère Lapin, Cox's Seafood Market, CudaCo., The Farmhouse at Serenbe, George & Pink's, The Gray, Husk Savannah, Indigenous, Jackrabbit Filly, Jewel of the South, Killer PoBoys, Miss River, NC Seafood Restaurant, Panini Pete's/PP Hospitality Group, Parkway Bakery & Tavern, Pêche, Saffron Nola, Saltbox Seafood Joint, Sandbar/Chiles Hospitality, Sanguich de Miami, Sea Wolf Tybee, Tryon Palace Seafood, Waterfront Seafood Shack Market & Eatery, The Wyld, Xin Chao.

To all the artisans and companies that are responsible for the tools and equipment we relied on throughout our creative process: Charleston Oyster Tables, Fontana Forni, Lettuce Grow, Middleton Made Knives, The Oyster Bed, Recteq, Sea Island Forge, Smithey Ironware, Toadfish.

To all the farms and institutions we visited and the producers of sustainable seafood that were a part of our journey, thank you for the rich and abundant education. Your impact is bountiful: Bluehouse Salmon, Gamble Creek Farms, Gilliard Farms, Louisiana Crawfish Co., Lowcountry Oyster Co., Maritime and Seafood Industry Museum (Biloxi), Murder Point Oysters, Open Blue Cobia, Pin Point Heritage Museum, Sea Love Sea Salt Co., Shogun Farms, South Carolina Aquarium, Sterling Caviar, Sun Shrimp, Sunburst Trout Farms, The Beach Institute African-American Cultural Center, University of Miami Rosenstiel School of Marine, Atmospheric, and Earth Science.

To our book team, thank you for answering our endless questions and guiding us through this project: Lisa Ekus, Sally Ekus, and the rest of The Ekus Group and Amy Marr, Debbie Berne, and the rest of the team at Weldon Owen. And, of course, our dear friend and photographer Ziv Sade.

To our restaurant teams at Preux & Proper and Joyce, thank you for pushing us forward, holding us up, and holding it down. In many ways, the creative process of this book started at Preux & Proper, and many of these recipes are now being executed on the highest level at Joyce. We'd be nowhere without the support, loyalty, and belief of these people: Javier Ascencio, Sasha Alcide, Kayleigh Coates, Spencer Emanuel, Tevon Garnett, Simon Garcia, Crystal Gutierrez, Dalton Holcombe, Shane Kirkland, Josh & Kat Kopel, Ross Knight, Angel Macias, Alix Marson, Alex Maumoynier, Rob Moss, Anthony Rayas, Eduardo Real, Prince & Athena Riley, Nate Santana, Bo Smothers, Paul Trevino, Nando Ventura, Anthony Valdovinos, Philip Villasenor.

ABOUT THE AUTHORS

Meet Sammy Monsour and Kassady Wiggins, a dynamic husband-and-wife duo whose culinary journey is a fusion of passion, innovation, and sustainability. Together, they are the creative force behind the acclaimed Joyce restaurant in downtown Los Angeles, where Southern charm meets modern coastal cuisine.

KASSADY WIGGINS, a seasoned beverage director and trailblazer in the craft cocktail scene, hails from Greenville, South Carolina. Influenced by her early exposure to organic farming and permaculture, she crafts Southern-inspired drinks that have been celebrated by *Eater*, *Forbes*, *LA Weekly*, *LA Magazine*, and *LA Times*. Her zero-landfill beverage program sparked a waste management system upgrade at their former restaurant Preux & Proper, earning them a Green Star from the City of Los Angeles.

SAMMY MONSOUR, a Michelin award-winning chef and food activist, brings a rich culinary heritage rooting from his parent's neighborhood restaurant in Chapel Hill, North Carolina. A graduate of the Culinary Institute of America and a third-generation chef, Sammy's restaurants in Boston and Los Angeles have earned acknowledgment and acclaim from James Beard Foundation, Eater National, and Zagat. Beyond the kitchen, Sammy's focus on sustainable food systems position him as a leading advocate, contributing to organizations like the Chefs Manifesto and Environmental Defense Fund, and serving on the boards of Chefs Collaborative and Smart Catch.

United by their love for food, beverage, culture, and travel, Kassady and Sammy have embarked on numerous adventures around the globe. From touring sustainable salmon farms in Norway to snorkeling in Nice, their experiences weave a rich tapestry that flavors their culinary narrative. Their commitment to sustainability and ocean conservancy is matched only by their passion for hospitality and togetherness. With a shared vision for the future, Sammy and Kassady continue to leave an indelible mark on the culinary landscape, showcasing their expertise, creativity, and dedication to sustainable hospitality.

weldonowen

an imprint of Insight Editions
PO Box 3088
San Rafael, CA 94912
www.weldonowen.com

Copyright © 2024 Weldon Owen
All rights reserved, including the right of
reproduction in whole or in part in any form.

ISBN-13: 979-8-88674-123-0

The information in this book is provided as a resource for inspiration and education. Author and Publisher expressly disclaim any responsibility for any adverse effects from the use or application of the information contained in this book. Neither the Publisher nor Author shall be liable for any losses suffered by any reader of this book.

CEO Raoul Goff
VP Publisher Roger Shaw
Associate Publisher Amy Marr
Publishing Director Katie Killebrew
VP Creative Chrissy Kwasnik
VP Manufacturing Alix Nicholaeff
Sr Production Manager Joshua Smith
Sr Production Manager, Subsidiary Rights
    Lina s Palma-Temena

Photography Ziv Sade & Sammy Monsour
Food & Beverage Styling Ziv Sade, Kassady Wiggins & Sammy Monsour
Designer Debbie Berne
Editor Amy Marr

Weldon Owen would also like to thank Rachel Markowitz, Elizabeth Parson, and Sharon Silva.

Printed in China
10 9 8 7 6 5 4 3 2 1

Insight Editions, in association with Roots of Peace, will plant two trees for each tree used in the manufacturing of this book. Roots of Peace is an internationally renowned humanitarian organization dedicated to eradicating land mines worldwide and converting war-torn lands into productive farms and wildlife habitats. Roots of Peace will plant two million fruit and nut trees in Afghanistan and provide farmers there with the skills and support necessary for sustainable land use.